Printed by Kiyanni B., Write It Out Publishing, LLC. in the United States of America.

Write It Out Publishing, LLC

Virginia Beach, Virginia

Writeitoutpublishing.com

ISBN: 979-8-9874539-8-8

Book Cover Illustrator: Maurice Rogers

Photographer: Anita Pearson Photography

Editor: Dina Reid & Tamira K. Butler-Likely

First printing, (e-book or paperback) March 2023

Sandra Pierce Mathis

Virginia Beach, VA 23464

spaulett55@gmail.com

A Resource Guide for Elementary Teachers

Children's Literature by Black Authors:

A Culturally Responsive Approach to Reading Instruction

Sandra Pierce Mathis, EdD

Write It Out
PUBLISHING, LLC

VIRGINIA BEACH, VA

A Resource Guide for Elementary Teachers

Children's Literature by Black Authors:

A Culturally Responsive Approach to Reading Instruction

Sandra Pierce Mathis, EdD

This book is dedicated to Black authors and illustrators of Children's Literature. May your voices be heard.

About This Resource Guide

by Sandra Pierce Mathis, EdD, author

In 1926, Dr. Carter G. Woodson founded Negro History Week with the purpose of celebrating the achievements of Black Americans. In February 1970, this became an annual month-long celebration. Dr. Woodson's overall purpose, however, was to inspire schools to teach students about the achievements of Black people all year long.

In 1990, the Black Caucus of the National Council of Teachers of English started the African American Read-In. The purpose of the African American Read-In was to make literacy a significant part of Black History Month, to celebrate Black writers, and to elevate Black experiences. Since that time, African American Read-Ins have been held all over this country during the month of February each year in schools, churches, coffee shops, community centers, kitchens, and living rooms, with the goal of celebrating Black authors.

More recently, schools across America have focused on the importance of meeting the diverse needs of all cultures represented in the classroom. This approach is referred to as culturally responsive teaching. Thus, the purposes of this instructional resource guide are as follows: to give teachers the opportunity to use literature by Black authors to teach reading comprehension skills in Pre-Kindergarten through grade 5, to teach genres, to provide more opportunities for children of color to see themselves and their life experiences reflected in children's literature, to provide a list of children's books with Black history themes that can be used throughout the year, and to enable teachers of all backgrounds to feel more comfortable and knowledgeable about diversity issues and specifically about Black history. Teachers could also use this list of books as a component of their classroom libraries. Finally, the content of these wonderful books will benefit students and teachers of all cultural backgrounds by building cultural awareness. Moreover, Black authors share a unique writing perspective and world view that will enlighten all readers.

The books listed as mentor texts under each skill area could also be used to teach more than one comprehension skill. You will note that in this resource guide, I have used selections to teach more than one reading comprehension skill. For example, a book listed under teaching the concept of main idea could also be used to teach author's purpose. In addition, examples of graphic organizers to enhance the acquisition of reading comprehension skills are found after each section. There are so many others.

Finally, and most importantly, I just want you, the teacher, to expose all children to the history and life experiences of Black Americans as expressed in more than 100 children's books annotated in this teacher's guide! The use of children's literature to teach reading comprehension skills could bridge cultural gaps, promote culturally responsive teaching in all areas of our country and throughout the world, aid in social-emotional learning, and increase understanding among children and teachers of various cultures and ethnicities within our schools. The use of children's literature by Black authors to teach in classrooms could fulfill the dream of Dr. Woodson and impact social change in America.

Enjoy the books and be inspired!

Contents

Teaching How to Determine the Main Idea

Teaching elementary students how to determine or find the main idea can be a very challenging endeavor. Although children are very skilled at providing details of a reading selection, many have difficulty stating what the book or passage is mostly about. This skill is very important because it bridges paragraph and essay development as well as the ability to summarize passages. When teaching this concept, be sure to ask the following questions:

Are there certain words and/or phrases that are repeated throughout the text? What do all of these repeated words or phrases tell you? What is the "Big Idea"? Main idea graphic organizers are quite beneficial in helping students improve in this skill area by providing a visual representation of the main idea and details.

1. *We Came to America* (Picture Book)

Faith Ringgold, author and illustrator

Publisher: Alfred A. Knopf (2016)

Genre: Nonfiction Picture Book

Summary: This nonfiction picture book is a tribute to every American who came before us. With immigration and diversity in America as timely themes, students will carry the message of diversity into our nation's future. After reading this book, the students will gain insight into how America was shaped. This book sends a great message to our children and youth.

Interest Level: Kindergarten – Grade 3

Reading Age: 5 – 8 years

2. *Rosa*

Nikki Giovanni, author

Bryan Collier, illustrator

Publisher: Henry Holt & Company (2007)

Genre: Nonfiction/Biography

Summary: This biography describes the life and experiences of Rosa Parks, Mother of the Civil Rights Movement. Mrs. Parks started this movement by not giving up her seat on a bus in Montgomery, Alabama, on Dec. 1, 1955.

Interest Level: Preschool – Grade 3

Reading Age: 4 – 8 years

3. *Before She Was Harriet*

Lesa Cline-Ransome, author

James Ransome, illustrator

Publisher: Holiday House, 2017

Genre: Nonfiction

Summary: Harriet Tubman was known by many names—Moses, General Tubman, Minty, Araminta, and then Harriet Tubman. Tubman served the roles of spy, liberator, and suffragist. This poem pays tribute to a true American hero with slavery and freedom as messages in this book. This is also an excellent book for teaching figurative language and the parts of speech, including nouns, verbs, prepositions, and adverbs. Your students will treasure this book!

Interest Level: Preschool – Grade 3

Reading Age: 4 – 8 years

4. *The People Could Fly* (The Picture Book)

Virginia Hamilton, author

Leo and Diane Dillon, illustrators

Publisher: Alfred A. Knopf, New York, 1985

Genre: Folktale

Summary: Considered an "extraordinary and moving" tale of Black folklore, this book will come to life in the mind of the reader. A group of slaves, unable to bear their treatment any longer, call upon the African magic that allows them to fly away. The triumph of the human spirit and the fight for freedom are themes in this book.

Interest Level: Grades 3 – 5

Reading Age: 8 – 10 years

5. *William and the Good Old Days*

Eloise Greenfield, author

Jan Spivey Gilchrist, illustrator

Publisher: Harper Collins, 1993, New York

Genre: Fiction

Summary: William is the young grandson in this book who is trying to cope with his grandmother's illness. He remembers his grandmother and all the things she could do before she became ill. As a result of her illness, William has a difficult time accepting the fact that his grandmother is sick and can't be herself. Many children who live with their grandparents or have a close relationship with them will be able to make a text-to-self connection with this story. Loss, sorrow, and hope are themes in this book.

Interest Level: Kindergarten – Grade 3

Reading Age: 5 – 8 years

6. *Not Quite Snow White*

Ashley Franklin, author

Ebony Glenn, illustrator

Publisher: Harper Collins, 2019, New York

Genre: Realistic Fiction

Summary: Tameika loves to dance and wants the role of Snow White, but after the audition, the other children begin to whisper that she is not right for the part. This saddens Tameika, who shares it with her mother. Read to find out if Tameika gets the part. The importance of self-confidence and what to do when that confidence is threatened are themes in this book. Children will gain insight regarding how to handle challenging situations in their lives.

Interest Level: Pre-Kindergarten – Grade 1

Reading Ages: 4 – 6 years

7. *America, My Love, America, My Heart*

Daria Peoples-Riley, author and illustrator

Publisher: Greenwillow Books, 2021

Genre: Fiction/Poem

Summary: A single question posed by children of color all across America is, "America, do you love me?" Based on the author's own experiences, this book inspires children of color to ask questions of America's acceptance, which is a theme in this book. Written in the format of a poem, thought provoking, and challenging, readers will examine their own personal beliefs and attitudes toward the many different colors of America. Children, adolescents, and adults will be able to make connections to this literary piece.

Interest Level: Pre-Kindergarten – Grade 3

Reading Ages: 4 – 8 years

8. *Just the Two of Us*

Will Smith, author

Kadir Nelson, illustrator

Publisher: Scholastic, Inc., 2001, New York

Genre: Nonfiction

Summary: Based on a song with the same title, the author, who is also a well-known actor, wrote this book as a tribute to his first-born son. In this story, he makes a promise to be a good father and a wonderful influence in his son's life. Dignity, integrity, and honor are themes in this book.

Interest Level: Pre-Kindergarten – Grade 3

Reading Ages: 4 – 8 years

Main Idea Hints
(Right in front of your eyes)

In general, the title of the article tells you the **TOPIC**.

In general, the sub-title of the article tells you the **MAIN IDEA**.

Then, the text & illustrations will tell you the **KEY DETAILS.** The key details are important facts AND supporting reasons (evidence) for the main idea, either stated explicitly or inferentially.

Then, a reader must determine the **BIG IDEA**, taking the topic, main idea and key details to determine what it all means, figuring out the **BIG DEAL** by thinking, asking & answering...
SO WHAT?
www.helloliteracy.blogspot.com

Polar Bears in Peril

Arctic sea ice is melting, making it harder for polar bears to survive in the wild

NOVEMBER 02, 2012 | By Elizabeth Winchester | 🖶 Print

JOHN BROWN—GETTY IMAGES

Polar bears' features help them survive in the Arctic. A thick layer of fat helps keep the bears warm.

http://www.timeforkids.com/news/polar-bears-peril/86701

RIT.2

I can explain how key details support the
MAIN IDEA

Title: _____

In one or two words, what is the article mostly about?

[box]

(a person, place, or thing or idea, process, event or concept)

and what about it?

[box]

and how do you know?

[four-column box]

Write a 10-word GIST statement below.

_____

_____

Hello Common Core Reading 3-5

he LO LITERACY

Teaching Characterization

The student will describe the characters' personal attributes and how those descriptions impact the problem and solution of the story. Teaching characterization also develops the student's knowledge of point of view in a story. In teaching point of view, a student determines if a story is written in first person, second person, or third person. Some words that may be used to describe character include brave, kind, mean, helpful, independent, and supportive. Students should also be able to give examples of a character's specific traits and how those traits impact the elements of a story. Children's books by Black authors tend to demonstrate specific character traits such as perseverance, resilience, determination, and the importance of overcoming challenges.

1. *I Am Enough*

   Grace Byers, author

   Keturo Bobo, illustrator

   Publisher: Balzer + Bray, 2018

   Genre: Nonfiction

Summary: The author of this book emphasizes that regardless of one's looks, abilities, or beliefs, every child is unique, able, and worthy of respect. The messages or themes in this book include encouragement, recognition of diversity, and showing respect and kindness to others. This is an excellent book for building self-confidence in children by teaching them to believe in themselves.

   Interest Level: Pre-Kindergarten – Grade 2

   Reading Ages: 3 – 7 years

2. *Gifts Are Given with Love*

Allyna Robinson Hughley, author

Arundoy Ghosh Biswas, illustrator

Publisher: Allyna Robinson Hughley, 2021

Genre: Realistic Fiction

Summary: A young girl learns that it's more important to receive gifts with love even if you don't get what you asked for. This is a great lesson in teaching children the true meaning of being appreciative. Love and gratefulness are themes in this book.

Interest Level: Pre-Kindergarten – Grade 2

Reading Ages: 4 – 9 years

3. *Mufaro's Beautiful Daughters*

John Steptoe, author

Publisher: Lothrop, Lee & Shepard Books, 1987

Genre: Fairy Tale

Summary: Set in Africa, two sisters, Manyara and Nyasha, are both outwardly very beautiful but have completely opposite personalities. Both daughters—one kind and one mean—go before the king, who will choose a wife. This engaging "Cinderella" story demonstrates how it pays to be a good, honest person.

Interest Level: Pre-Kindergarten – Grade 5

Reading Ages: 3 – 10 years

4. *Of Thee I Sing* (A Letter to My Daughters)

Barack Obama, author

Loren Long, author

Publisher: Alfred A. Knopf, New York, 2010

Genre: Nonfiction

Summary: President Obama has written a beautiful, heartwarming letter to his daughters. He lets them know that there are no boundaries and that they can achieve and become anything they want with hard work and determination, just like many who came before them. Pursuing one's dreams is a theme in this book.

Interest Level: Pre-Kindergarten – Grade 4

Reading Age: 3 – 9 years

5. *Little Dreamers* (Visionary Women Around the World)

Vashti Harrison, author and illustrator

Publisher: Little, Brown and Company, 2018

Genre: Nonfiction

Summary: In this great book, Vashti Harrison highlights the true stories of thirty-five successful women from all over the world. Inventors, scientists, artists, and writers are all presented in a very engaging format for the reader. What a great piece of literature for motivating young girls to succeed in life! Inspiration and creativity are themes in this book.

Interest Level: Pre-Kindergarten – Grade 4

Reading Age: 2 – 9 years

6. *Each Kindness*

Jacqueline Woodson, author

E.B. Lewis, illustrator

Publisher: Nancy Paulsen, 2012

Genre: Realistic Fiction Picture Book

Summary: A new girl arrives at school and none of the students welcome her or include her in any of the activities. The teacher takes the time to talk with her class about the importance of being kind to others. Teaching students about the impact of rejection and the importance of welcoming a new student and making friends are themes in this book. These messages are so important in teaching social skills in our schools today.

Interest Level: Kindergarten – Grade 5

Reading Age: 5 – 10 years

7. *Jesse Owens* (Legendary Track Star)

Fred and Patricia McKissack, authors and illustrator

Publisher: Enslow Elementary, 2013

Genre: Nonfiction/ Biography

Summary: Jesse Owens always loved running and as a boy could outrun all of his playmates. He eventually competed in the Summer Olympics in Berlin, Germany. Later, Jesse earned four Olympic Gold Medals in track and field events, which showed the world that Adolph Hitler's theory of racial inferiority was inaccurate. In this book, Jesse Owens demonstrates excellent character traits in addition to the great attributes of an Olympic Star athlete. Perseverance is a theme in this book.

Interest Level: Grades 1 – 2

Reading Age: 6 – 8 years

8. *Hidden Figures – The True Story of Four Black Women and the Space Race*

Margot Lee Shetterley and Winifred Conkling, authors

Laura Freemen, illustrator

Publisher: Scholastic, 2019

Genre: Nonfiction

Summary: Based on the New York Times bestseller, Hidden Figures, this book tells the inspiring story of four Black women who helped NASA launch men into space. Dorothy Vaughan, Mary Jackson, Katherine Johnson, and Christine Darden were really good at math. They provided calculations for America's first journeys into space, during a time when being Black and a woman placed limitations on what they could do. Working hard and persistence are themes in this book that will inspire students to see the value of math beyond the classroom.

Interest Level: Grades 1 – 5

Reading Age: 6 – 10 years

9. *For the Love of the Game* (Michael Jordan and Me)

Eloise Greenfield, author

Jan Spivey Gilchrist, illustrator

Publisher: HarperCollins, 1997

Genre: Fiction

Summary: This inspiring poem encourages children to view life with the same determination that Michael Jordan displayed on the basketball court. In this book, two children parallel their goals with the outstanding abilities of Michael Jordan. Goal setting and believing that you have the power within you to accomplish your goals and your dreams are the themes of this book.

Interest Level: Grades 1 – 5

Reading Age: 6 – 10 years

10. *The Undefeated*

Kwame Alexander

Kadir Nelson, author

Publisher: Houghton Mifflin Harcourt, 2019

Genre: Nonfiction/Poetry

Summary: Historically, this book highlights different aspects of Black life in America, including slavery and the Civil Rights Movement. Resilience and perseverance are themes as the author pays tribute to some of the greatest heroes who ever lived. The vivid descriptions of each famous individual will enable young readers to fully grasp a wide range of character traits.

Interest Level: Kindergarten and up

Reading Age: 5 years and up

11. *Salt in His Shoes: Michael Jordan in Pursuit of a Dream*

Deloris Jordan with Roslyn M. Jordan, authors

Kadir Nelson, illustrator

Publisher: Simon & Schuster Books for Young Readers, 2000

Genre: Fiction

Summary: As a child, Michael was ready to give up his dream of becoming a basketball player. He thought he would not grow tall enough. Michael's parents stepped in and shared valuable life lessons with him. In this book, Michael is taught to rely on determination, patience, and prayer in his quest to become taller and to become a good basketball player.

Interest Level: Kindergarten – Grade 5

Reading Age: 5 – 10 years

12. *I Got Next*

Daria Peoples-Riley, author and illustrator

Publisher: Greenwillow Books, New York, 2019

Genre: Realistic Fiction

Summary: In this book, a young basketball player practices on the playground. As he prepares for an upcoming pickup game, his shadow urges him to play hard and leave his heart on the court. He continues to dribble, shoot, and score, and his shadow gives him the encouragement he needs to go out and give his all in competing with others. Hard work, determination, and imagination are themes in this book.

Interest Level: Pre-Kindergarten – Grade 5

Reading Age: 4 – 10 years

13. *I'm Gonna Push Through*

Jasmyn Wright, author

Shannon Wright, illustrator

Publisher: Atheneum Books for Young Readers, Simon & Schuster, New York, 2020

Genre: Nonfiction

Summary: Believing in yourself and never giving up are themes in this book. Illustrations of famous individuals from all backgrounds who succeeded by never giving up are presented. This is a great book for building self-esteem and self-confidence.

Interest Level: Pre-Kindergarten – Grade 3

Reading Age: 4 – 8 years

14. *Dancing in the Wings*

Debbie Allen, author

Kadir Nelson, illustrator

Publisher: Dial Books for Young Readers, New York, 2000

Genre: Fiction

Summary: At first, Sassy doesn't feel that she is acceptable as a ballerina because of her big feet, too long legs, and even her big mouth. Later, when a director of an important dance festival comes to her class, her talent is revealed and Sassy steps out of those wings and shines above the rest! Self-confidence is a powerful theme in this book.

Interest Level: Kindergarten – Grade 5

Reading Age: 5 – 10 years

15. *Dorothea Lange* (The Photographer Who Found the Faces of the Depression)

Carole Boston Weatherford, author

Sarah Green, pictures

Publisher: Albert Whitman & Company, Chicago

Genre: Nonfiction

Summary: Carole Weatherford captures the life and dedication of Dorothea Lange, who took photos of the Great Depression. The world was captivated by these photos. As a result of being stricken with polio and developing a limp, Dorothea was sensitive to those who suffered in any way. This is a great mentor text for character analysis. Compassion for others is a theme in this book.

Interest Level: Kindergarten – Grade 5

Reading Age: 4 – 10 years

16. *Ruby Bridges Goes to School* (My True Story)

Ruby Bridges, author

Publisher: Scholastic, Inc. New York, 2003

Genre: Autobiography

Summary: Ruby Bridges tells her story of becoming the first Black child to enter school during a period of intense segregation. The children attending the school were all white and left school because of her. However, the children later returned and Ruby was able to make friends with some of them. This is a story of true bravery.

Interest Level: Kindergarten – Grade 2

Reading Age: 4 – 8 years

Character Traits

How is my character as a person?

nice	mean	sad
bright	angry	antisocial
cheerful	bossy	comfortless
caring	cruel	depressed
charming	dark	down
considerate	disrespectful	friendless
delightful	evil	gloomy
encouraging	harsh	glum
friendly	hateful	heartbroken
kind	impolite	heavy-hearted
likable	insensitive	hopeless

positive	negative
cooperative	uncooperative
calm	reactive
dependable	undependable
fair	unfair
honest	dishonest
humble	conceited
mature	immature
patient	impatient
responsible	irresponsible
trustworthy	untrustworthy

Name: Period:

Characterization

Directions: There are four ways in which an author develops characters.
1. Physical description of the character
2. The character's words and actions
3. What others say about the character
4. Direct commentary about the character by the narrator

Write the character's name in the center then find an instant of each type of characterization.

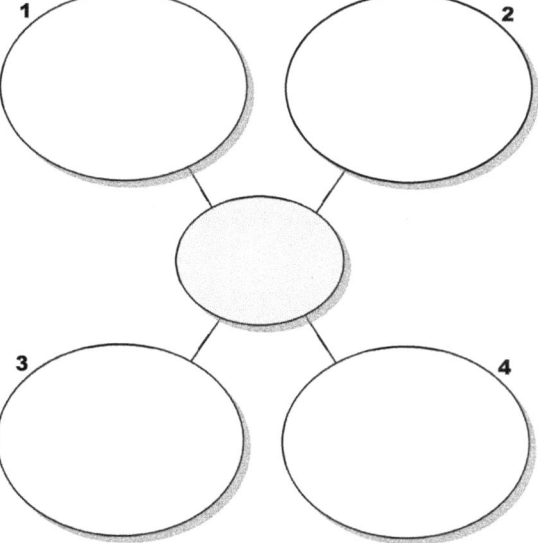

© Freeology.com

Teaching Making Inferences/Drawing Conclusions

Making inferences is an abstract reading strategy and a very important skill in improving reading comprehension. Very often, important concepts are not stated in a text, so children have to use their background knowledge along with information in the text to infer or draw a conclusion. We call this deductive reasoning. Ask your students this question: Based on what you have read, what else is probably true? Based on the background and experiences of the children in your classroom, answers will certainly vary. The books listed in this section will provide opportunities for children to improve in the skill of making inferences, which also help students with drawing conclusions.

1. *The Patchwork Quilt*

Valerie Flournoy, author

Jerry Pinkney, illustrator

Publisher: Dial Books for Young Readers, 1985

Genre: Realistic Fiction

Summary: Tanya and her grandmother are making a quilt. While making it, Tanya realizes through her grandmother that a quilt tells a life story. This warm-hearted story about family relations in a multigenerational family will teach children the value of forming bonds with older relatives. The love of family is a theme in this story.

Interest Level: Kindergarten – Grade 3

Reading Age: 4 – 8 years

2. *Tar Beach*

Faith Ringgold, author and illustrator

Publisher: Crown Publishing, 1991

Genre: Fantasy

Summary: A young girl named Cassie dreams to be free to go wherever she wants to go. The roof top of her family's apartment building becomes "tar beach." The stars lift her up and she flies over the city, claiming the buildings as her own. The wish for freedom is a message in this book.

Interest Level: Grades 1 – 4

Reading Age: 6 – 9 years

3. *The Magician's Hat*

Malcolm Mitchell, author

Joanne Lew-Vriethoff, illustrator

Publisher: Orchard Books, 2018

Genre: Fantasy

Summary: A magician introduces children to the power of books. He invites them to reach into his hat to pull out whatever they find when they dig down deep. An afternoon at the library leads children to discover the magic of books and that dreams can become a reality through those books.

Interest Level: Pre-Kindergarten – Grade 3

Reading Age: 4 – 8 years

4. *The Hundred Penny Box*

Sharon Bell Mathis

Leo & Diane Dillon, illustrators

Publisher: Puffin Books, 1975

Genre: Realistic Fiction

Summary: Michael's love for his great-great-aunt, who lives in the house with him, creates a conflict with his mother, who wants to get rid of all the great-great-aunt's old belongings. The hundred penny box is one of the things the mother wants to throw away. Read to find out why this item is so special to the great-great-aunt. The love of family, care, and support are strong messages in this wonderful story.

Interest Level: Kindergarten – Grade 5

Reading Age: 5 – 9 years

5. *The Gold Cadillac*

Mildred D. Taylor, author

Michael Hays, illustrator

Publisher: Dial Books for Young Readers, 1987

Genre: Fiction

Summary: A strain is placed on a family when the husband purchases a gold Cadillac without first consulting with his wife. The children are proud of their new car and the family takes it for a drive to the south. For the first time, after driving the Cadillac to show it off, the family experiences racism. Race relations is a theme in this book. Facing racial prejudice is a theme in this book.

Interest Level: Grades 4 and 5

Reading Age: 10 – 11 years

6. *Talk About a Family*

Eloise Greenfield, author

James Calvin, illustrator

Publisher: HarperTrophy, 1978

Genre: Realistic Fiction

Summary: Genny hopes that her brother's return from the army will stop her parents from fighting all the time. However, when the fighting doesn't stop, Genny is angry. A family learns that just because there are changes that occur within the family structure, it doesn't have to be a bad thing. Love in the midst of family conflict is a theme in this story.

Interest Level: Grades 2 – 4

Reading Age: 7 – 9 years

Making Inferences

Directions: Inferences involve drawing conclusions and making judgments based on facts and evidence. Write important details and facts in the boxes on the left. Write inferences about those important details in the boxes on the right.

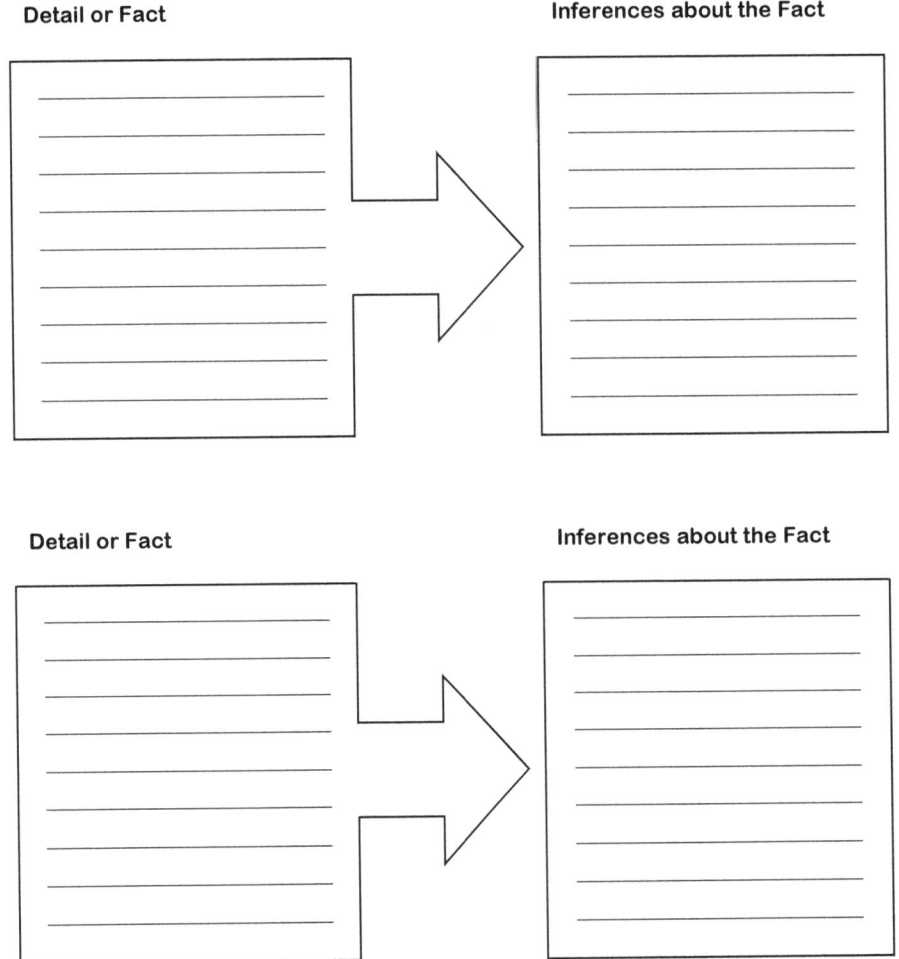

Detail or Fact   **Inferences about the Fact**

Detail or Fact   **Inferences about the Fact**

© Freeology.com

Teaching Sequencing

The skill of sequencing is used throughout a student's day from the time he or she arises in the morning until they go to bed at night. All individuals have to maintain schedules of some sort, which is a form of sequencing. Ask your students if they can tell, in order, the most important events that happened in a story. The skill of sequencing is also important in summarizing a story—being able to tell the most important events in order. This skill is necessary in mastering concepts in social studies and science as well as in practical applications such as following a recipe.

1. *Time for Kenny*

Brian Pinkney, author and illustrator

Publisher: Harper Collins, 2021

Genre: Fiction

Summary: This story is all about Kenny's day. Wearing the right outfit, learning to play soccer, and getting ready for bed are all part of Kenny's day. A very nice book for the very young child that teaches the sequencing skill.

Interest Level: Pre-Kindergarten – Grade 1

Reading Age: 4 – 6 years

2. *This is the Rope* (A Story from the Great Migration)

Jacqueline Woodson, author

James Ransome, illustrator

Publisher: Candlewick Press, 2019

Genre: Fiction

Summary: This is a story about one family's journey north during the Great Migration that starts with a little girl in South Carolina who finds a rope under a tree one summer. This rope becomes part of her family history. From the early 1900s until the mid-1970s, more than six million African Americans moved from the rural south to northern cities. This book pays tribute to those generations of families. The importance of knowing one's family history is a theme in this book.

Interest Level: Kindergarten – Grade 3

Reading Age: 5 – 8 years

3. *Freedom Soup*

Tami Charles, author

Jacqueline Alcantara, illustrator

Publisher: Candlewick, 2019

Genre: Historical Fiction

Summary: Every year, Haitian's all over the world ring in the new year by eating a special soup. In this story, a Haitian grandmother and granddaughter share a holiday, a family recipe, and a story of freedom. Passing down cultural traditions from one generation to the next is a theme in this book.

Interest Level: Kindergarten – Grade 5

Reading Age: 5 – 10 years

4. *Jesse Owens* (Legendary Track Star)

Fred and Patricia McKissack, authors and illustrator

Publisher: Enslow Elementary, 2013

Genre: Nonfiction/ Biography

Summary: Jesse Owens always loved running and as a boy could outrun all of his playmates. He eventually competed in the Summer Olympics in Berlin, Germany. Later, Jesse earned four Olympic Gold Medals in track and field events, which showed the world that Adolph Hitler's theory of racial inferiority was inaccurate. An excellent story about the life of Jesse Owens, students will learn details of his early life, his upbringing, and how he was inspired to become an Olympic track star. Hard work and perseverance despite the odds are themes in this book.

Interest Level: Kindergarten – Grade 5

Reading Age: 5 – 10 years

5. *Marian Anderson* (A Great Singer) Revised Edition

Patricia and Frederick McKissack

Publisher: Enslow Publishers, 2001

Genre: Biography

Summary: Marian Anderson's life and upbringing in Philadelphia is told in the finest of details by Patricia and Frederick McKissack. Young readers will gain knowledge of how a very gifted singer succeeded in spite of the odds against her because of her race. Perseverance and hard work are themes in this wonderful story.

Interest Level: Grades 3 – 5

Reading Age: 8 – 10 years

6. *Cooking with Love: Just Like My Mama Taught Me* (Authentic Virginia Cuisine)

Sandra Paulette Pierce Mathis, author

Publisher: Xlibris, 2020

Genre: Nonfiction/Cookbook

Summary: This book contains recipes that were taught by the author's mother and were passed down from previous generations, including the author's grandmother and great-grandmother, who were all Virginia natives. Love and wisdom for life are also included with a quote by the author's mother at the beginning of each chapter. Excellent recipes and words of wisdom that will nourish the body, soul, and spirit are found in this book. A loving relationship developed between a mother and daughter is a pervasive theme in this book.

Interest Level: Kindergarten – Grade 5

Reading Age: 5 – 10 years

7. *Preaching to the Chickens: The Story of Young John Lewis*

Jabari Asim, author

E. B. Lewis, illustrator

Publisher: Nancy Paulsen Books, 2016

Genre: Nonfiction/Biography

Summary: Young John Lewis dreamed of being a preacher. While growing up on a farm in Alabama, each child in his household had a chore and feeding the chickens belonged to John. John forms a bond with the chickens by emulating what he heard and saw at his church with the chickens! Aspiration is a theme in this book.

Interest Level: Kindergarten – Grade 3

Reading Age: 5 – 8 years

8. *Mary McLeod Bethune: A Great American Educator*

Patricia C. McKissack, author

Publisher: Regensteiner Publishing Enterprises, Inc., 1985

Genre: Biography

Summary: This is a great story of how Mary McLeod Bethune, a great educator, rose from humble beginnings in the cotton fields of South Carolina. Her career advanced to the role of college president and as presidential advisor to US President Franklin Delano Roosevelt. Readers will be inspired by Bethune's devotion and dedication to the field of education.

Interest Level: Grades 4 – 6

Reading Age: 9 – 12 years

9. *The Bell Rang*

James Ransome, author and illustrator

Publisher: Atheneum Books for Young Readers, 2019

Genre: Historical Fiction

Summary: Every morning, the plantation overseer rings a bell and a young slave girl experiences the same daily routine. One day, however, her brother ran to freedom. She is then torn between wanting her brother back and letting him be free. Hope and courage are themes in this wonderful book.

Interest Level: Kindergarten – Grade 3

Reading Age: 5 – 8 years

10. *Mae Among the Stars*

Roda Ahmed, author

Stasia Burrington, illustrator

Publisher: HarperCollins Children's Books, 2018

Genre: Biography

Summary: This book tells the real-life story of Mae Jemison, the first African American woman in space. Mae followed her childhood dreams with support from both of her parents, who believed in her, taught her to believe in herself, and encouraged her to pursue her dreams no matter the opinions of others. (This would also be an excellent mentor text used to teach character traits.) The fulfillment of one's dreams is a theme in this book.

Interest Level: Pre-Kindergarten – Grade 2

Reading Age: 4 – 6 years

11. *Kamala Harris* (Rooted in Justice)

Nikki Grimes, author

Laura Freeman, illustrator

Publisher: Atheneum Books for Young Readers, Simon & Schuster, New York, 2020

Genre: Biography

Summary: This is the life story of Kamala Harris, the first woman of color to serve as Vice President of the United States. This biography is in a picture book format and is suitable for any age or grade level. The book begins with her parents' ancestry. Her experiences during her youth and college life are also included. Readers will enjoy this book about Vice President Harris. Achieving success is a theme in this book. This is a great story for all young girls of color.

Interest Level: Pre-Kindergarten – Grade 7

Reading Age: 4 – 12 years

12. *Sisters & Champions* (The True Story of Venus and Serena Williams)

Howard Bryant, author

Floyd Cooper, illustrator

Publisher: Philomel Books, New York, 2018

Genre: Biography

Summary: No one thought these two sisters would be successful in tennis. They were laughed at every time their father talked about how successful they would become someday. With hard work and determination, these two sisters have beat the odds. An inspiration for young people, the two sisters are also best friends with a deep love for each other.

Interest Level: Kindergarten – Grade 5

Reading Age: 5 – 10 years

13. *Before She Was Harriet*

Lesa Cline-Ransome, author

James E. Ransome, illustrator

Publisher: Holiday House Book, New York, 2017

Genre: Biography/Poem

Summary: Harriet Tubman was known by several names before she took the name Harriet. Those names were Moses, General Tubman, Minty, and Araminta. Harriet also served the following roles: spy, liberator, and suffragist. This biography/poem pays tribute to a true American hero.

Interest Level: Pre-Kindergarten – Grade 4

Reading Age: 4 – 9 years

14. *Can't Scare Me* (Trickster Tales)

Ashley Bryan, author and illustrator

Publisher: Atheneum Books for Young Readers, New York, 2013

Genre: Trickster Tale

Summary: This is a tale about a fearless little boy who defies his grandmother's warnings about one, two, and three-headed giants. One day he goes off by himself and he's not scared one bit but realizes he misses his grandma. Read to see what happens next!

Interest Level: Pre-Kindergarten – Grade 4

Reading Age: 4 – 9 years

15. *Ella Fitzgerald: The Tale of a Vocal Virtuoso*

Andrea Davis Pinkney

Brian Pinkney, illustrator

Publisher: Jump at the Sun Hyperion Books for Children, New York, 2002

Genre: Biography

Summary: This is an interesting story about the life of Ella Fitzgerald who began her life as a singer on the stage of the Apollo theater when she was just seventeen years old. Several surprising facts about her will entice young readers to want to know more about this famous singer's life and influences.

Interest Level: Kindergarten – Grade 5

Reading Age: 5 – 10 years

16. *Jump at the Sun*

Alicia D. Williams, author

Jacqueline Alcantara, illustrator

Publisher: Simon & Schuster, New York, 2021

Genre: Biography

Summary: Zora Neale Hurston, a great folklorist and writer, is celebrated in this book, which chronicles her early beginnings as an author and collector of stories. In this book for children, Hurston is celebrated as an extraordinary writer who changed the face of American literature.

Interest Level: Pre-Kindergarten – Grade 3

Reading Age: 4 – 8 years

Process Chart

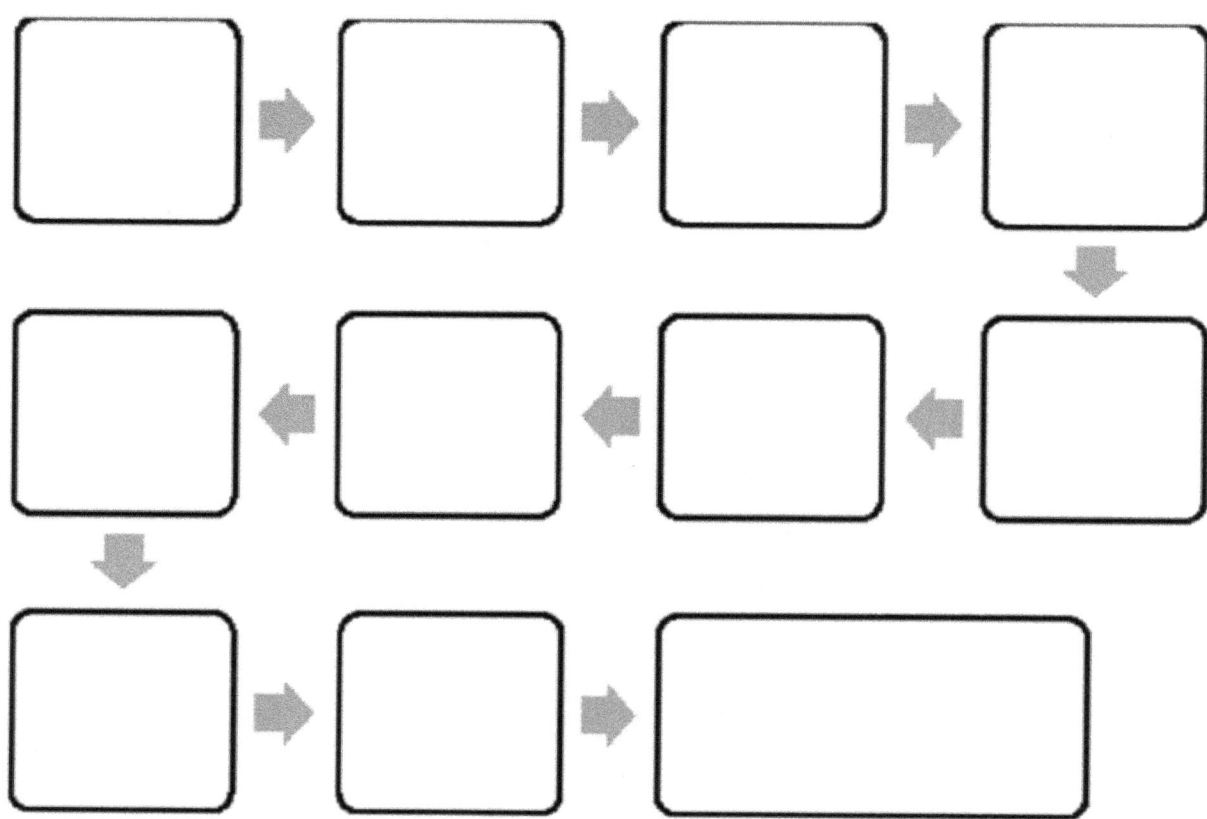

Vocabulary and Word Study: Teaching Base Words, Prefixes, Suffixes and Parts of Speech

When students learn the meanings of base words, prefixes, suffixes, and know the parts of speech, their vocabulary skills are strengthened. Students who are unable to decode and break words into syllables have a difficult time with reading requirements in the upper grades as vocabulary becomes more complex. The books annotated in this section support the instruction of these specific word study skills.

1. *The Undefeated*

Kwame Alexander, author

Kadir Nelson, illustrator

Publisher: Houghton Mifflin, 2019

Genre: Nonfiction

Summary: The author wrote this poem mainly to inspire and encourage Black communities. It pays tribute to Black people from the past and from all walks of life. In addition, this book is an excellent mentor text for word study. It provides examples of multisyllabic words containing base words, prefixes, and suffixes while teaching character traits and the parts of speech. What an excellent resource for third and fourth-grade students who need practice with these skills! Every teacher will want this book in their classroom library.

Interest Level: Kindergarten – Grade 5

Reading Age: 5 – 10 years

2. *Ambitious Girl*

Meena Harris, author

Marissa Valdez, illustrator

Publisher: Little, Brown & Company, 2021

Genre: Fiction

Summary: The power of dreaming big is the message or theme of this book. It celebrates girls and lets them know that it is fine to have ambition. At the same time, this story uses many adjectives to describe how girls become ambitious. It's all about believing in yourself!

Interest Level: Pre-Kindergarten – Grade 3

Reading Age: 3 – 8 years

3. *I Am Brown*

Ashok Banker, author

Sandhya Prabhat, illustrator

Publisher: Lantana Publishing, United Kingdom; Lerner Publishing Services, Minneapolis, Minnesota, 2020.

Genre: Fiction

Summary: Being brown is highly celebrated in this book. Brown is everything and there are no limits. This is a must read for any child of color anywhere in the world! It is also an excellent mentor text for teaching the parts of speech and building vocabulary through the use of the following: common nouns, proper nouns, pronouns, action and state of being verbs, and adjectives. Being proud of who you are is a theme in this book.

Interest Level: Kindergarten – Grade 3

Reading Age: 5 – 8 years

4. *Time for Kenny*

Andrea Davis Pinkney and Brian Pinkney, authors and illustrators

Publisher: Greenwillow Books, 2021

Genre: Fiction

Summary: This simple book for the very young child is all about Kenny's day. The author guides the reader through a typical day of a young child—deciding what to wear, overcoming fears, and playing soccer are some examples. Children will easily make connections to this book. This book is useful for teaching the parts of speech.

Interest Level: Pre-Kindergarten – Grade 1

Reading Age: 4 – 6 years

5. *Black Is a Rainbow Color*

Angela Joy, author

Ekua Holmes, illustrator

Publisher: Ekura Brook Press

Roaring Brook Press, New York, 2020

Genre: Fiction

Summary: In this book, a child reflects on the meaning of being Black. This book describes Black in every way possible and points out that Black is a culture as well as a color. Black also comes in all shades, which form a rainbow of colors. Being proud of who you are is a theme in this book.

Interest Level: Pre-Kindergarten – Grade 3

Reading Age: 3 – 8 years

Teaching Author's Purpose

Why did the author write this? Was it written to persuade, to inform, or to entertain (PIE)? Elementary students are often taught the PIE acronym as a mnemonic to help them remember the three main purposes that an author has for writing. Writing to persuade means to try to get the reader to believe, think, feel, or do something. To inform includes providing facts and information to the reader. To entertain includes the use of humor, narration, or storytelling. The books included in this list provide excellent examples for teaching author's purpose.

1. *Roll of Thunder, Hear My Cry*

Mildred Taylor, author

Frontispiece, Jerry Pinkney

Publisher: Puffin Books, 1991, New York

Genre: Historical Fiction

Summary: During the span of one year, the Logan family encounters many struggles that would challenge anyone—night riders and embarrassment are just two examples. In the midst of all this turmoil, Cassie learns the importance of owning land and having a place to call their own. As a result, the family is able to maintain a sense of pride and dignity.

Interest Level: Grade 5 and up

Reading Age: 10 years and up

2. *Freedom over Me* (Eleven Slaves, Their Lives and Dreams Brought to Life) by Ashley Bryan

Ashley Bryan, author and illustrator

Publisher: Atheneum Books for Young Readers, New York, 2016

Genre: Historical Fiction

Summary: Mr. Bryan describes the lives of eleven slaves, their emotions, skills, dreams, and desires for freedom. Although the value of the enslaved was purely based upon what each was worth in monetary value, the author presents each slave as a real person with hopes and desires for the future. The power of dreams is a theme in this book.

Interest Level: Grades 4 – 5

Reading Age: 9 – 10 years

3. *My Brother, Charlie*

Holly Robinson Peete, Ryan Elizabeth Peete, and Deneen Milner

Shane W. Evans, Illustrator

Publisher: Scholastic Press, New York, 2010

Genre: Fiction

Summary: Based on the life of the author's son, who has autism, she and her daughter, Ryan Elizabeth Peete, share their experiences about Charlie. In this story, Ryan and Charlie are twins. Ryan describes ways in which Charlie is different but also how he excels in so many aspects that other children might not. This book was written to help families who are struggling with understanding autism. Celebrating differences is one theme in this book. In addition to author's purpose, this book is a great text for teaching the skill of compare and contrast.

Interest Level: Pre-Kindergarten – Grade 4

Reading Age: 4 – 9 years

4. *Don't Touch My Hair*

Sharee Miller, author and illustrator

Publisher: Little, Brown Books for Young Readers, 2019

Genre: Realistic Fiction

Summary: Aria is an African American girl with 'big' hair, but doesn't want people touching it. Everywhere she goes, someone wants to touch her hair. Written with humor, this book will entertain while teaching readers to respect personal space, to ask permission, and how to maintain boundaries.

Interest Level: Pre-Kindergarten – Grade 2

Reading Age: 4 – 6 years

5. *Bedtime Bonnet*

Nancy Redd, author

Nneka Myers, illustrator

Publisher: Random House Children's Books, 2020

Genre: Realistic Fiction

Summary: An entertaining but realistic story about African American families "putting up their hair" at night and "taking it down in the morning" with the use of a night head covering such as a bonnet. This is the first time a children's book has been written on the topic of nighttime Black hair routines that are common among all members of a Black family. Children and adults alike will love this book! Black students in your class will make a real connection to this story!

Interest Level: Preschool – Grade 2

Reading Age: 3 – 6 years

6. *Off to See the Sea*

Nikki Grimes, author

Elizabeth Zunon, illustrator

Publisher: Sourcebooks, Jabberwocky, Naperville, Illinois

Genre: Fantasy

Summary: Written for ages 4 and up, this book tells the adventures of bath time for little ones and what it takes to get Mommy's little ones clean! In this magical story, the bathtub becomes the sea. A fun story that children will absolutely adore and will want it repeatedly read to them! The power of imagination is the pervasive theme in this book.

Interest Level: Kindergarten – Grade 3

Reading Age: 5 – 8 years

7. *The Animal Market* (A Book to Read and to Color)

Joyce R. Wilkins, author

Edeltraub Hawkins, illustrator

Publisher: Donning Productions, Norfolk, 1993

Genre: Realistic Fiction

Summary: Sammy has vivid dreams of all the wonderful things he would like for Christmas. The dreams include getting something special for his mother. After finding the gifts he had dreamed about hidden in his closet, Sammy believes that wishes come true!

Interest Level: Kindergarten – Grade 3

Reading Age: 5 – 8 years

8. *Rhythm Ride* (A Road Trip Through the Motown Sound)

Andrea Davis Pinkney, author

Publisher: Roaring Book Press, New York, 2015

Genre: Nonfiction

Summary: The purpose of this book is to inform the reader of the inspiring story of Motown. It is a story in which most African Americans can easily connect. Although the Motown story began in 1959, the music is still popular to this very day. It is still played on the airwaves and its story and music are shared with younger generations of Black children by their parents and grandparents. Music as an inspiring legacy is the theme of this book.

Interest Level: Grade 5

Reading Age: 10 years

9. *Kid President's Guide to Being Awesome*

Brad Montague and Robby Novak, authors

Publisher: Harper, 2015, New York

Genre: Nonfiction

Summary: Written to inspire children to be awesome, this book is entertaining, funny, and at the same time, so full of truths. It is also a motivator and children will enjoy this book. I'm sure they have seen Kid President at one time or the other through some of today's media platforms.

Interest Level: Grades 3 – 5

Reading Age: 8 – 10 years

10. *Ruth and the Green Book*

Calvin Alexander Ramsey with Gwen Strauss, authors

Floyd Cooper, illustrator

Publisher: Carolrhoda Books, Minneapolis, 2010

Genre: Historical Fiction

Summary: This story takes place in the 1950s during the Jim Crow era when segregation is legal. Ruth and her family travel from Chicago to Alabama to visit her grandmother. Along the way, the family is not welcome in restaurants and hotels. Finally, a friendly gas station attendant sells the family a copy of The Green Book, which lists safe places for travel. Read to find out how this pamphlet helps the family along the way and if the family makes it safely to Grandma's house. This is a very informative book for students as well as for teachers.

Interest Level: Kindergarten – Grade 5

Reading Age: 5 – 10 years

Name _____   Date_____

Title of Book/Poem _____

The author is trying to teach us that _____

_____

_____

_____ .

I know this because _____

_____

_____

_____ .

Draw an important scene from the book that is **evidence** of what the author is trying to teach:

Determing Author's Purpose/Fiction   © K. Moulihos

Teaching Compare and Contrast

Compare and contrast enables students to see how characters, conflicts, and solutions can be the same or different within the same book or in more than one reading selection. Compare means to tell how things are alike and contrast means to tell how things are different. The Venn Diagram is a very common graphic organizer used to display this skill. You will find an example of a Venn Diagram at the end of this section.

1. *The Day You Begin*

Jacqueline Woodson, author

Rafael Lopez, illustrator

Publisher: Nancy Paulsen Books, 2018

Genre: Realistic Fiction

Summary: A new student at school thinks she is different and doesn't fit in with the other students, only to discover that things begin to change when she shares her story. A beautiful book that teaches each student that he or she is important regardless of background, culture, race, or socioeconomic status.

Interest Level: Kindergarten – Grade 3

Reading Age: 5 – 8 years

2. *Just Like a Mama*

Alice Faye Duncan, author

Charnelle Pinkney Barlow, illustrator

Publisher: Simon & Schuster Books for Young Readers, 2019

Genre: Realistic Fiction

Summary: A little girl wants to live with her parents; instead, she lives with Mama Rose, who is just like a mama to her. Mama Rose does all the things her mother would do for her. Later, she realizes that Mama Rose loves her and she loves Mama Rose. Many children who don't live with biological parents but are being reared by someone who loves them will relate well to this book. Love is the theme in this book.

Interest level: Kindergarten – Grade 3

Reading Age: 4 – 8 years

3. *Pecan Pie Baby*

Jacqueline Woodson, author

Sophie Blackall, illustrator

Publisher: Penguin Young Readers Group, 2010

Genre: Fiction

Summary: Gia is tired of hearing about the new baby that hasn't even been born yet. This is the story of a little girl trying to adjust to conflicting emotions when everyone keeps talking about the impending arrival of the new baby. Children with younger siblings will definitely make a personal connection to this story. Making adjustments and accepting changes in life are themes in this book.

Interest Level: Kindergarten – Grade 3

Reading Age: 5 – 8 years

4. *My Brother Charlie*

Holly Robinson Peete, Ryan Elizabeth Pete with Deneen Milner, authors

Shane Evans, illustrator

Publisher: Scholastic Press, Inc. New York, 2010

Genre: Fiction

Summary: Based on the life of this author's son, who has autism, she and her daughter, Ryan Elizabeth Peete, share their experiences about Charlie. In this story, Ryan and Charlie are twins. Ryan describes ways in which Charlie is different but also how he excels in so many ways that other children might not. This book was written to help families who are struggling with understanding autism. Celebrating differences is one theme in this book. In addition to author's purpose, this book is a great text for teaching the skill of compare and contrast.

Interest Level: Pre-Kindergarten – Grade 4

Reading Age: 4 – 9 years

Name

My Character and I Comparison

Directions: On the left side, write characteristics for the main character in your story. On the right side, write characteristics for you. In the middle, write the characteristics you and your character share.

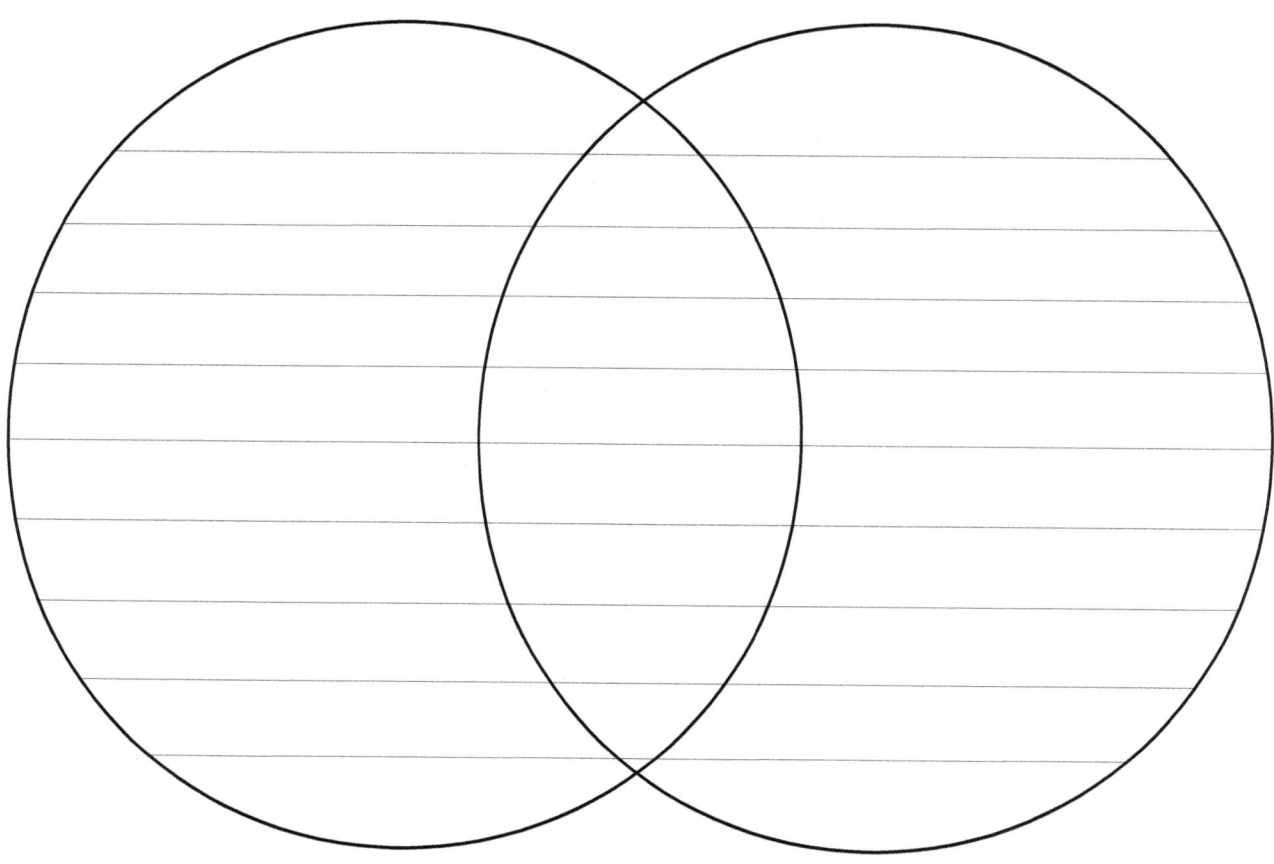

Teaching the Theme of a Story

The theme of a story is the underlying message that the author wants to convey. By contrast, the main idea is what the story is mostly about. More often than not, our elementary students often confuse main idea and theme. To clarify the differences, we might ask our students: "What lesson does the author want us to learn from this story?" Themes are used to share important ideas and messages about issues that face the characters and the setting of a story.

1. *Fifty Cents and a Dream: Young Booker T. Washington*

Jabari Asim

Bryan Collier, illustrator

Publisher: Little, Brown and Company, 2012

Genre: Biography

Summary: This picture book biography describes the life of young Booker T. Washington and the fulfillment of his dream to receive an education. Readers will be inspired by what Washington set out to accomplish and the great things that unfolded. Although this book can serve as a great mentor text for characterization and sequencing, ask the students to tell you the theme. After reading this book, readers will gain a great respect for Booker T. Washington and the person he was determined to become.

Interest Level: Kindergarten – Grade 3

Reading Age: 4 – 8 years

2. *I Believe*

Grace Byers, author

Keturah A. Bobo, illustrator

Publisher: Balzer + Bray, An Imprint of Harper Collins Publishers, 2020

Genre: Nonfiction

Summary: A follow-up to I Am Enough, this is a book that shares with the reader that they can become anything they want to become if only they believe they can. Written as a poem, with children in active roles and in various careers, Ms. Byers once again encourages children to value themselves and not let anything hold them back.

Interest Level: Kindergarten – Grade 3

Reading Age: 4 – 8 years

3. *The Bench*

Meghan, The Duchess of Sussex, author

Christian Robinson, illustrator

Publisher: Random House Publishers, 2021, New York

Genre: Realistic Fiction

Summary: This story was written on Father's Day by the author, The Duchess of Sussex, to her husband, shortly after the birth of their son. The bench is a special place where a father and son spend a lot of time. A special relationship between a father and son is shared in this book. Cultivating a good relationship with a parent or parents would be a theme in this book.

Interest Level: Pre-Kindergarten – Grade 5

Reading Age: 4 – 10

4. *Moses* (When Harriet Tubman Led Her People to Freedom)

Carole Boston Weatherford, author

Kadir Nelson, illustrator

Publisher: Hyperion Books, New York, 2006

Genre: Picture Book/Biography

Summary: A fine tribute to Harriet Tubman, this book honors her legacy. In this book, the author tells the story of her nineteen trips north to carry the enslaved to freedom. Harriet is seen as Moses in the Bible. She had faith in God. Bravery and perseverance are themes in this book.

Interest Level: Pre-Kindergarten – Grade 3

Reading Age: 4 – 8 years

5. *He's Got the Whole World in His Hands*

Kadir Nelson, author and illustrator

Publisher: Dial Books for Young Readers, New York, 2005

Genre: Song Lyrics/Picture Book

Summary: The title of this book was taken from a popular spiritual of the same name. The author takes a popular spiritual and transforms it into a picture book with messages of faith, diversity, and living in community. All three of these great messages are themes in this book.

Interest Level: Kindergarten – Grade 5

Reading Age: 5 – 10 years

6. *Sojourner Truth's Step-Stomp Stride*

Andrea Davis Pinkney, author

Brian Pinkney, illustrator

Publisher: Disney's Jump at the Sun Books, New York, 2009

Genre: Biography

Summary: Readers will find this life story to be engaging and enlightening. It elaborates on the bravery of this former slave woman who could neither read nor write but spoke her mind! Readers and listeners alike will be inspired by her demands for equal rights for Blacks and women. Bravery is a theme in this story.

Interest Level: Kindergarten – Grade 3

Reading Age: 5 – 8 years

7. *Nelson Mandela*

Kadir Nelson, author and illustrator

Publisher: Katherine Tegen Books, 2013, New York

Genre: Biography

Summary: Readers will learn the meaning of the term "apartheid" and will be captivated by the story of Nelson Mandela and his fight for freedom. In this book, children will witness a true example of an individual who devoted himself to fighting for the equal rights of all people regardless of the color of their skin. Justice is a theme in this book.

Interest Level: Kindergarten – Grade 5

Reading Age: 5 – 10 years

Name: _____   Date: _____

Discovering the THEME of a Literary Work

Title	What is the significance of the title?
How	How does the main character change? How is this change brought about?
Emotions	What emotions did you feel at the end?
Mood	What was the mood of the story (sad, uplifting, sentimental, etc...)?
Enduring	What message from the story applies to life?

www.teachingresourceresort.blogspot.com

Teaching Setting

The setting of a story is its time and place. The setting is one of the elements of a story and lays its foundation. It is among the first clues the reader/listener receives as to what lies ahead. Before reading a selection, teachers might ask students to be prepared to answer the following questions: "What are the time and place of this story?" "How does the setting influence the conflict and the resolution?"

1. *Harlem Renaissance Party*

Faith Ringgold, author and illustrator

Publisher: HarperCollins, 2015

Genre: Historical Fiction

Summary: Lonnie and his uncle return to Harlem in the 1920s and meet famous writers, musicians, artists, and athletes such as Langston Hughes, Zora Neale Hurston, and many others. Young readers will learn about the significance of this important era in African American history.

Interest Level: Preschool – Grade 5

Reading Age: 3 – 10 years

2. *Coming on Home Soon*

Jacqueline Woodson, author

E.B. Lewis, illustrator

Publisher: Penguin, 2004

Genre: Historical Fiction

Summary: Ada Ruth stays behind with Grandma while her mother goes to work in Chicago. It's war time and women are needed to fill men's jobs while men are away fighting. Ada Ruth misses her mother and desires for her to come home. Children whose parents are often deployed will easily make a personal connection with this book. Dealing with the absence of a parent is a theme in this book.

Interest Level: Pre-Kindergarten – Grade 5

Reading Age: 4 – 10 years

3. *Neeny Coming, Neeny Going*

Karen English, author

Paintings by Synthia Saint James

Publisher: Bridgewater Paperbacks, 1997

Genre: Realistic Fiction

Summary: Essie is anxious for the arrival of her cousin, Neeny, to return to the island on which she was raised. When Neeny arrives, Essie finds Neeny no longer interested in the island way of life. Essie is disappointed but finds a way to keep the island close to her cousin's heart. Forgetting one's roots is a theme in this story.

Interest Level: Pre-Kindergarten – Grade 3

Reading Age: 4 – 8 years

4. *Freedom in Congo Square*

Carole Boston Weatherford, author

R. Gregory Christie, illustrator

Publisher: Little Bee Books, Bonner Publishing Company, New York, 2016

Genre: Nonfiction Picture Book

Summary: Based on a little known piece of African American history, this book is written in the format of a poem. It describes the freedom that slaves experienced only on Sundays in New Orleans' Congo Square. On Sundays, the slaves would dance, sing, and play music together. On that day only, the slaves felt free from oppression. Freedom is a theme in this book.

Interest Level: Kindergarten – Grade 5

Reading Age: 5 – 10 years

5. *Sit-In: How Four Friends Stood Up by Sitting Down*

Andrea Davis Pinkney, author

Brian Pinkney, illustrator

Publisher: Little, Brown and Company, New York, 2010

Genre: Nonfiction Picture Book

Summary: Four young college students were the first to peaceably protest against segregation at a Woolworth's Department Store Lunch Counter in 1960. This picture book tells the story of how these four young men followed in the footsteps of Dr. Martin Luther King Jr. and made a significant contribution to the fight for racial equality and the Civil Rights Movement in America.

Interest Level: Grades 1 – 5

Reading Age: 6 – 10 years

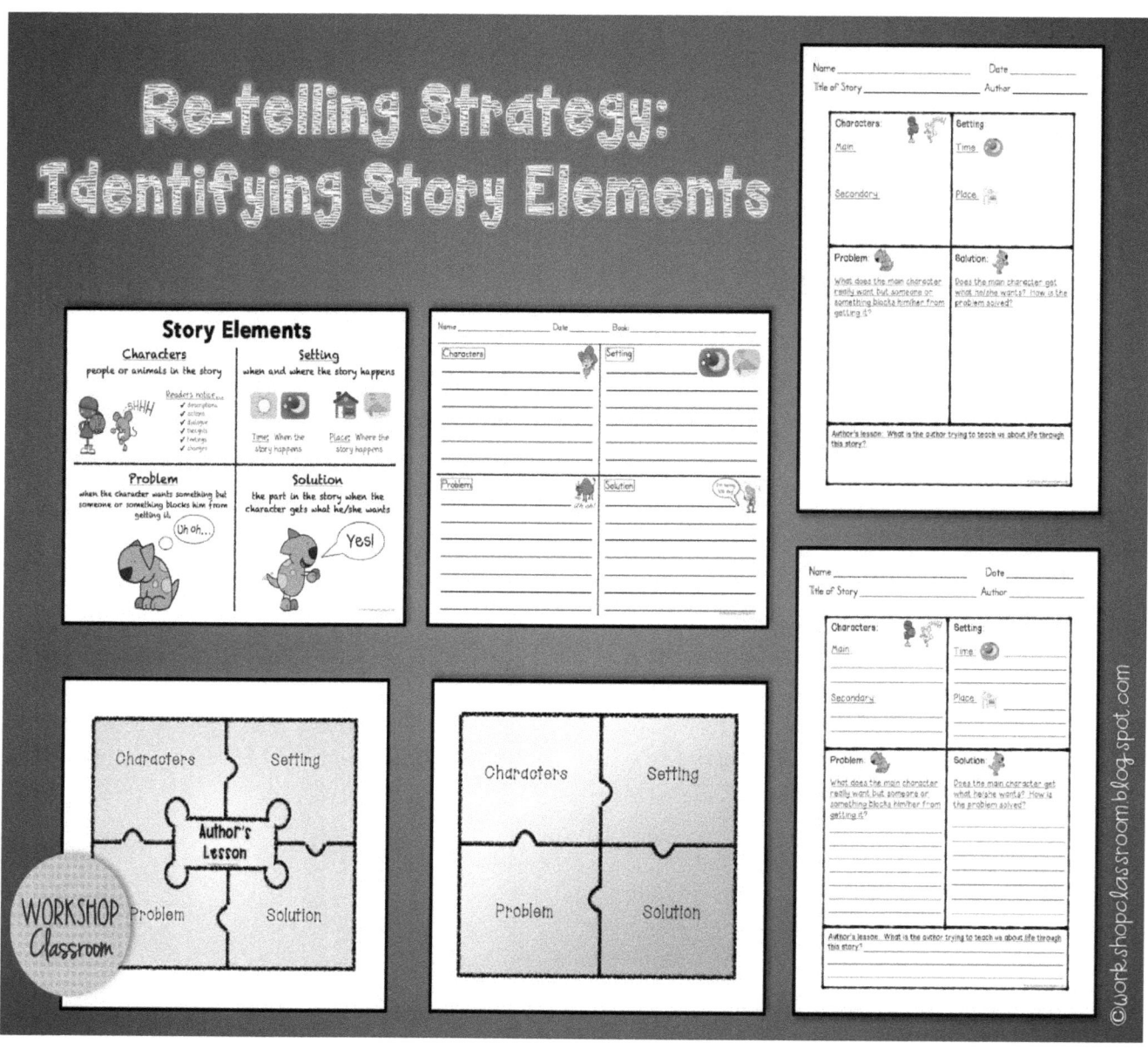

Teaching Cause and Effect

A cause was the reason something happened. It answers the question: Why did this happen? An effect is the result. It answers the question: What happened? Words like because of, why, since, and as a result, often signal a cause and effect relationship. Moreover, understanding cause and effect is an important life skill for students. The books in this annotated list are excellent examples of cause and effect relationships.

1. *Why Should I Go to School?*

Sandra Pierce Mathis, author

Publisher: Xlibris, 2019, Bloomington, Indiana

Genre: Nonfiction Picture Book

Summary: Achieving an education opens doors of opportunity and at the same time enables children to make a difference in the world. This book asks a question that often resonates in the minds of many young people. It starts by presenting practical suggestions for how to prepare for school each day and moves on to presenting faces of famous people of color who succeeded in life by going to school. What it takes to become successful is an important theme in this book.

Interest Level: Kindergarten – Grade 5

Reading Age: 5 – 10 years

2. *This is the Rope*

Jacqueline Woodson, author

James Ransome, illustrator

Publisher: Nancy Paulsen Books, 2013

Genre: Historical Fiction

Summary: During The Great Migration of 1910–1970, millions of African American families left the south and headed north seeking better opportunities. This is the story of one family's journey north during the Great Migration. A little girl in South Carolina finds a rope under a tree one summer, but has no idea that the rope will become part of her family's history.

Interest Level: Kindergarten – Grade 5

Reading Age: 5 – 10 years

3. *Why the Sun and the Moon Live in the Sky*

Elphinstone Dayrell, author

Blair Lent, illustrator

Publisher: Scholastic, Inc. New York, 1968

Genre: Folktale

Summary: This story tells how Sun and Moon built a house and invited Water. Water kept coming in and consumed their space until Sun and Moon had to go live in the sky. Hospitality is one theme in this book. Children and adults alike will be intrigued by the African illustrations throughout the book!

Interest Level: Pre-Kindergarten – Grade 5

Reading Age: 4 – 10 years

4. *Sulwe*

Lupita Nyong'o, author

Vashti Harrison, illustrator

Publisher: Simon & Schuster, 2019

Genre: Fantasy

Summary: Sulwe means star. Being teased for being very dark, Sulwe wishes for her skin to be lighter. Later, she discovers that there is so much beauty in this world and inside of oneself. Sulwe urges the reader to learn to love and treasure oneself.

Interest Level: Pre-Kindergarten – Grade 3

Reading Age: 4 – 8 years

5. *Rosa*

Nikki Giovanni, author

Bryan Collier, illustrator

Publisher: Henry Holt and Company, 2005

Genre: Biography

Summary: A great mentor text for teaching the cause and effect skill, this book tells the story of Rosa Parks, Mother of the Civil Rights Movement. Mrs. Parks started a movement when she refused to give up her seat on a bus in Montgomery, Alabama on December 1, 1955. Standing up for what you feel is right is a theme in this book.

Interest Level: Kindergarten – Grade 5

Reading Age: 5 – 10 years

6. *More than Anything Else*

Marie Bradby, author

Chris K. Soentpiet, illustrator

Publisher: Scholastic, 1995, New York

Genre: Fiction

Summary: In this work of fiction, nine-year-old Booker T. Washington wants to learn to read more than anything else. However, he fears that working in the salt mines will prevent him from reaching his goal. His intense desire to learn to read will be an inspiration to young children today.

Interest Level: Kindergarten – Grade 4

Reading Age: 5 – 9 years

7. *Freedom's School*

Lesa Cline-Ransome, author

James Ransome, illustrator

Publisher: Disney Jump at the Sun, Los Angeles, 2015

Genre: Historical Fiction

Summary: After the slaves were freed, they were determined to learn how to read and to get a good education. Readers will get a real understanding of the intense desire and risks that were taken because of the desire of freed slaves who really wanted to go to school. Told from the perspective of a girl named Rosa, readers will enjoy this book and find great examples of the cause and effect skill in reading comprehension.

Interest Level: Kindergarten – Grade 5

Reading Age: 5 – 10 years

8. *Beat the Story-Drum, Pum-Pum*

Retold by Ashley Bryan, author and illustrator

Publisher: Atheneum Books for Young Readers

Genre: African Folktales

Summary: Folktales are stories passed on by word of mouth or a legend or myth shared among a people of culture. Five Nigerian folktales are presented in this rhythmic picture book. Readers will enjoy the language as well as the outstanding art work! The stories are both humorous and delightful!

Interest Level: Grades 3 – 7

Reading Age: 8 – 12 years

9. *Trombone Shorty*

Troy Andrews, author

Bryan Collier, illustrator

Publisher: Abrams Books for Young Readers, 1st Edition (April 14, 2015)

Genre: Autobiography

Summary: This book tells the life story of Troy Andrews, an American musician, also known as Trombone Shorty. A child music prodigy, Trombone Shorty was leading his own band by the age of six. The main focus of this book is about his life growing up in New Orleans where there was lots of early exposure to music. Readers will find relevant examples of cause and effect in this book.

Interest Level: Pre-Kindergarten – Grade 3

Reading Age: 4 – 8 years

10. *Gordon Parks* (How the Photographer Captured Black and White America)

Carole Boston Weatherford, author

Publisher: Jamey Christoph, Albert Whitman & Company, Chicago, Illinois

Genre: Nonfiction

Summary: This biography tells the story of the life of Gordon Parks. Mr. Parks had a huge impact on the world as a photographer, writer, filmmaker, musician, and poet who used his camera to take a stand against racism. Gordon faced many challenges, but he was determined to do well and he succeeded. A great text for teaching the cause and effect skill needed to improve reading comprehension.

Interest Level: Kindergarten – Grade 5

Reading Age: 4 – 10 years

11. *Please, Puppy, Please*

Spike Lee and Tonya Lewis Lee, authors

Kadir Nelson, illustrator

Publisher: Simon & Schuster Books for Young Readers, New York, 2005

Genre: Fiction

Summary: Two children try to get their puppy to obey them. Although this book was written for the very young child and emerging readers, practical examples of cause and effect are found here. Children of all ages might enjoy this book with its simple message and beautiful art work!

Interest Level: Pre-Kindergarten – Grade 3

Reading Age: 4 – 8 years

Name: _____ Date: __/__/____

Cause and Effect

(The cause is why it happened, and the effect is what happened.)

Topic: _____

Cause		Effect
_____ _____	⇒	_____ _____
Cause		Effect
_____ _____	⇒	_____ _____
Cause		Effect
_____ _____	⇒	_____ _____
Cause		Effect
_____ _____	⇒	_____ _____

www.free-printable-paper.com

Teaching Figurative Language

The use of figurative language makes colorful and interesting stories. Figurative language enables students to think beyond literal interpretations to grasp meanings. Some examples of figurative language include similes, metaphors, puns, alliterations, personifications, allusions, and idioms. Similes and metaphors make unlikely comparisons with the use of "like" or "as" (similes) and "is" (metaphors). Puns are the humorous use of words in a way as to suggest two or more of its meanings or the meaning of another word. Assigning human qualities to something other than a person is the use of personification. Allusions are implied or indirect references in literature. Idioms are commonly used groups of words that have a meaning that cannot be deducible from those individual words (e.g., raining cats and dogs). Readers will enjoy finding examples of figurative language in the following books.

1. *Be A King* (Dr. Martin Luther King, Jr.'s Dream and You)

Carole Boston Weatherford, author

James E. Ransome, illustrator

Publisher: Bloomsbury USA Children, 2018

Genre: Realistic Fiction

Summary: The author of this book challenges children of this generation to live as Dr. King would want them to live by following his principles of justice and equality. The text as well as the illustrations enable readers to learn about the life of Rev. Dr. King and how they, too, can be a "king" by following in Dr. King's footsteps. Excellent examples of figurative language are found in this book.

Interest Level: Kindergarten – Grade 5

Reading Age: 5 – 10 years

2. *Just Like a Mama*

Alice Faye Duncan, author

Charnelle Pinkney Barlow, illustrator

Publisher: Simon & Schuster Books for Young Readers, 2019

Genre: Realistic Fiction

Summary: A little girl wants to live with her parents; instead, she lives with Mama Rose, who is just like a mama to her. Mama Rose does all the things her mother would do for her. Later, she realizes that Mama Rose loves her and she loves Mama Rose. Many children who don't live with biological parents but are being reared by someone who loves them will relate well to this book. Good examples of figurative language are found in this delightful book with its overall love theme.

Interest level: Kindergarten – Grade 3

Reading Age: 5 – 8 years

3. *Just a Lucky So and So: The Story of Louis Armstrong*

Lesa Cline-Ransome, author

James Ransome, illustrator

Publisher: Holiday House, New York, 2016.

Genre: Biography

Summary: This book tells the life story of Louis Armstrong, also known as "Satchmo," in a very interesting yet simple way. Children will gain knowledge of who he was and his place in the history of African Americans. This famous musician succeeded against incredible odds. Good examples of similes are found in this book.

Interest Level: Kindergarten – Grade 5

Reading Age: 5 – 10 years

4. *Dreams for a Daughter*

Carole Boston Weatherford, author

Brian Pinkney, illustrator

Publisher: Atheneum Books for Young Readers, 2021

Genre: Realistic Fiction

Summary: Mothers encouraging their daughters to follow their dreams no matter what challenges they might face is the lesson in this book. For ages 4 through 8, excellent examples of similes and metaphors can be used to teach the important skill of explaining some of the many facets of figurative language.

Interest Level: Kindergarten – Grade 5

Reading Age: 5 – 10 years

5. *Firebird*

Misty Copeland, author

Christopher Myers, illustrator

Publisher: GP Putnam's Sons, 2014

Genre: Nonfiction/biography

Summary: With an abundance of similes and metaphors, this debut picture book by Misty Copeland, an American ballet dancer, is about a young girl who discovers herself through dance. In this story, she becomes the mentor for a fragile young girl who needs to gain confidence in herself and Misty shows her how to accomplish that. Gaining confidence and believing in yourself are themes in this book.

Interest Level: Kindergarten – Grade 5

Reading Age: 5 – 10 years

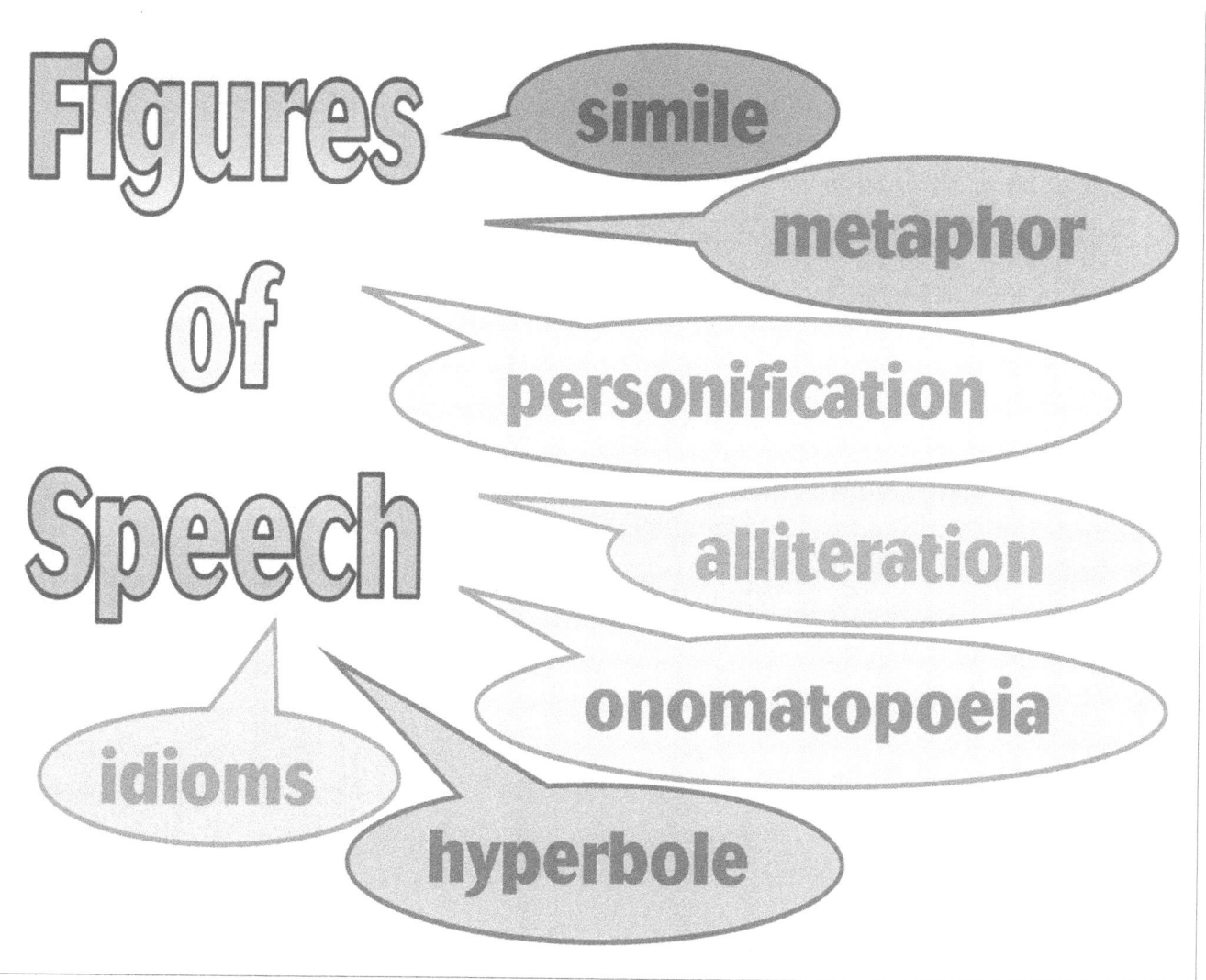

Teaching Nonfiction Text Features

Nonfiction text features include bolded words, captions, italics, headings and subheadings, maps, photos, table of contents, indices, and appendices. Students should become knowledgeable of these specific features, which will improve comprehension in skills such as determining fact versus opinion and fiction versus nonfiction. These are skills that can be difficult to grasp for young readers in early elementary grades.

1. *A Child's Introduction to African American History* (The Experiences, Events, and People that Shaped Our Country)

Jabari Asim

Lynn Gaines, illustrator

Publisher: Hachette Book Group, 2018

Genre: Nonfiction

Summary: If you've always wanted to gain more knowledge of the history of African Americans, this is the book for you! This comprehensive history of African Americans from the slave trade to the millennium is written in an easy-to-read format with 100 colorful illustrations is for children of all ages! This book should have a place in every teacher's classroom library! Lots of text features are found in this book.

Interest Level: Grades 3 – 7

Reading Age: 8 – 12 years

2. *We Are the Ship* (The Story of Negro League Baseball)

Kadir Nelson, author and painter

Publisher: Jump at the Sun Hyperion, New York, 2008

Genre: Nonfiction

Summary: The author tells the origin of Negro League Baseball and how it all started in the 1920s. This book will appeal to sports lovers of all ages. Readers will gain an understanding of what these gifted Black athletes had to endure in spite of their unmatched talents on the field. Nonfiction text features include photos, captions, and bold print. Determination despite the odds against you is a theme in this book.

Interest Level: Grades 4 and up

Reading Age: 9 years and up

Teaching with Novels (Chapter Books) and Nonfiction Books

Using novels for reading instruction is an excellent method for teaching reading comprehension. A novel is a fictitious prose of book length containing several chapters. Children become acquainted with chapter books or novels as early as second grade. However, the books become lengthier with more chapters by third grade. Many of the books listed in the previous sections were picture books. Novels and chapter books, such as biographies, provide the opportunity for teachers to teach all of the previous skills that have been mentioned in this resource guide: determining the main idea, making inferences/drawing conclusions, cause and effect, sequencing, and vocabulary development. Whether teachers choose to read a novel to the class or form groups or literature circles based on students' interests, novel studies are just another fun and interesting method of exposing students to excellent reading material.

Please use the following questions/skills to guide your discussion of each novel below. When using these strategies, your students will gain a much greater understanding of what they read and as a result, many reluctant readers will demonstrate more interest in reading novels or chapter books. The following questions can be utilized in the format of a graphic organizer or guided reading questions.

Making Predictions – What do you think will happen in this story?

Making Connections – Can I make a personal connection (text to self) to this story or book? Have I read another book that reminds me of this book (text to text)? What connection can I make with this text to something happening in the world (text to world)?

Visualizing – While reading this book, what pictures do I see in my mind?

Asking Questions While Reading – While reading, be sure to ask yourself questions such as "What if?"

Context Clues – While reading, take note of what is stated in an entire sentence or paragraph to denote meaning.

Summarizing – Somebody Wanted But So Then (SWBST) is an excellent and simple means of summarizing a fictional story. When summarizing nonfiction books use the 5 Ws method – Who was in the story? What happened? When did the story take place? Where does the story take place? Why or How was the problem or conflict resolved?

Plot – What happened in the beginning, in the middle, and at the end of the story?

Theme – What lesson does the author want me to learn from this story?

Point of View – What is the narrator's position in relation to the story being told? Is this story told in first person, second person, or third person?

Setting – What are the time and place in which this story happens?

Problem/conflict – What is the problem faced by the main character in the story?

Resolution – How was the problem resolved?

1. The Watsons Go to Birmingham – 1963

Christopher Paul Curtis, author

Publisher: Penguin Random House, 1995

Genre: Historical Fiction Novel

Summary: Byron is the oldest child in the Watson family of Flint, Michigan. He becomes difficult to handle so his parents decide to take Byron to Alabama to live with his grandmother. This unforgettable journey to Birmingham, Alabama, leads them into one of the darkest moments in American history. Readers and listeners will gain knowledge and understanding of issues in this country that took place during the Civil Rights Movement.

Interest Level: Grade 5 and up

Reading Age: 10 years and up

2. *Bud, Not Buddy*

Christopher Paul Curtis, author

Publisher: Delacorte Press (A Division of Random House), New York, 1999

Genre: Historical Fiction

Summary: Bud, a ten-year-old homeless child, spent several years in foster care. After the death of his mother, Bud sets out on his own to find his father, and what an adventure! This is truly an unforgettable story that students will want to read again and again! This story's setting is during the Great Depression, so students will gain knowledge of what was actually taking place in the lives of Americans during that time.

Interest Level: Grades 3 – 5

Reading Age: 8 – 10 years

3. *Roll of Thunder, Hear My Cry*

Mildred Taylor, author

Frontispiece, Jerry Pinkney

Publisher: Puffin Books, 1991, New York

Genre: Historical Fiction

Summary: During the span of one year, the Logan family encounters many struggles that would challenge anyone—night riders and embarrassment are just two examples. In the midst of all this turmoil, Cassie learns the importance of owning land and having a place to call their own. As a result, the family is able to maintain a sense of pride and dignity. This book is a great novel for the teacher to read aloud or to assign to reading groups.

Interest Level: Grade 5

Reading Age: 10 years

4. *The Mighty Miss Malone*

Christopher Paul Curtis, author

Publisher: Yearling, 2012, New York

Genre: Historical Fiction

Summary: In this story, an African American family struggles during the Great Depression. Deza is the smartest girl in her class and she loves her teacher. However, things begin to change when Father has to leave their home in Indiana to find work. Deza, Jimmie, Peg, and Roscoe are a close-knit family that endures many challenges. Readers won't be able to put this book down. Attempting to rise above family obstacles and changes in family dynamics is a theme in this book.

Interest Level: Grades 4 and up

Reading Age: 9 years and up

5. Gifted Hands, Revised Kids Edition: The Ben Carson Story

Gregg Lewis and Deborah Shaw Lewis, authors

Publisher: Zonderkidz Biography Publishing, 2014

Genre: Nonfiction/Autobiography

Summary: This is the powerful story of Dr. Ben Carson, the neurosurgeon who separated conjoined twins. Dr. Carson was raised in the inner city of Detroit, Michigan, by an uneducated mother who sacrificed so much to ensure that her two sons received the best education. Many elementary students will readily relate to how Ben was a failing student, needed glasses to improve his vision, and how his mother got him to learn his multiplication facts. Love, faith, and hard work are themes in this book.

Interest Level: Grades 3 – 5

Reading Age: 8 – 10 years

6. *One Crazy Summer*

Rita Williams-Garcia, author

Publisher: Amistad Publishers, 2010

Genre: Historical Fiction

Summary: Three sisters—Delphine, Vonetta, and Fern—travel to Oakland, California, from Brooklyn, New York, during the summer of 1968 to meet the mother who abandoned them seven years prior. When they arrive in Oakland, they discover that their mother is nothing like they imagined her to be. The girls don't get to visit Disneyland or any of the places in California that they thought they would visit. Read to find out where their mother sent them every day! There are several themes in this book with resilience being one of them.

Interest Level: Grades 4 – 5

Reading Age: 9 – 10 years

7. *We Beat the Street* (How a Friendship Pact led to Success)

The Three Doctors: Drs. Sampson Davis, George Jenkins, and Rameck Hunt with Sharon Draper, authors

Publisher: Puffin Books, 2005

Genre: Nonfiction/Biography

Summary: Three African American male doctors describe their journey from living on the streets of Newark, New Jersey, to their graduation from medical school to their employment as physicians. What a captivating story for children who live with the same challenges faced by these three extraordinary young men who rose above the lures of drugs and violence to become medical doctors in the same town in which they grew up. Readers and listeners alike will gain wisdom from these three as they share pitfalls, challenges, and the tenacity to overcome them.

Interest level: Grade 5 and up

Reading Age: 10 years and up

8. *A Friendship for Today*

Patricia McKissack, author

Allford Trotman Associates, cover photo

Elizabeth B. Parisi, cover design

Publisher: Scholastic, Inc., 2007

Genre: Fiction

Summary: Rosemary is faced with the challenge of being among the first African American students in her town to enroll in what had been an all-white school. As a result, Rosemary faces many challenges, including relationships with peers, a friend who becomes ill, and racism toward herself and her family. The theme of this story is friendship. Your students will really enjoy this book and will be able to make personal, text-to-text, and world connections to this story.

Interest Level: Grades 3 and up

Reading Age: 8 years and up

Book Review

I can give my opinion about a book.

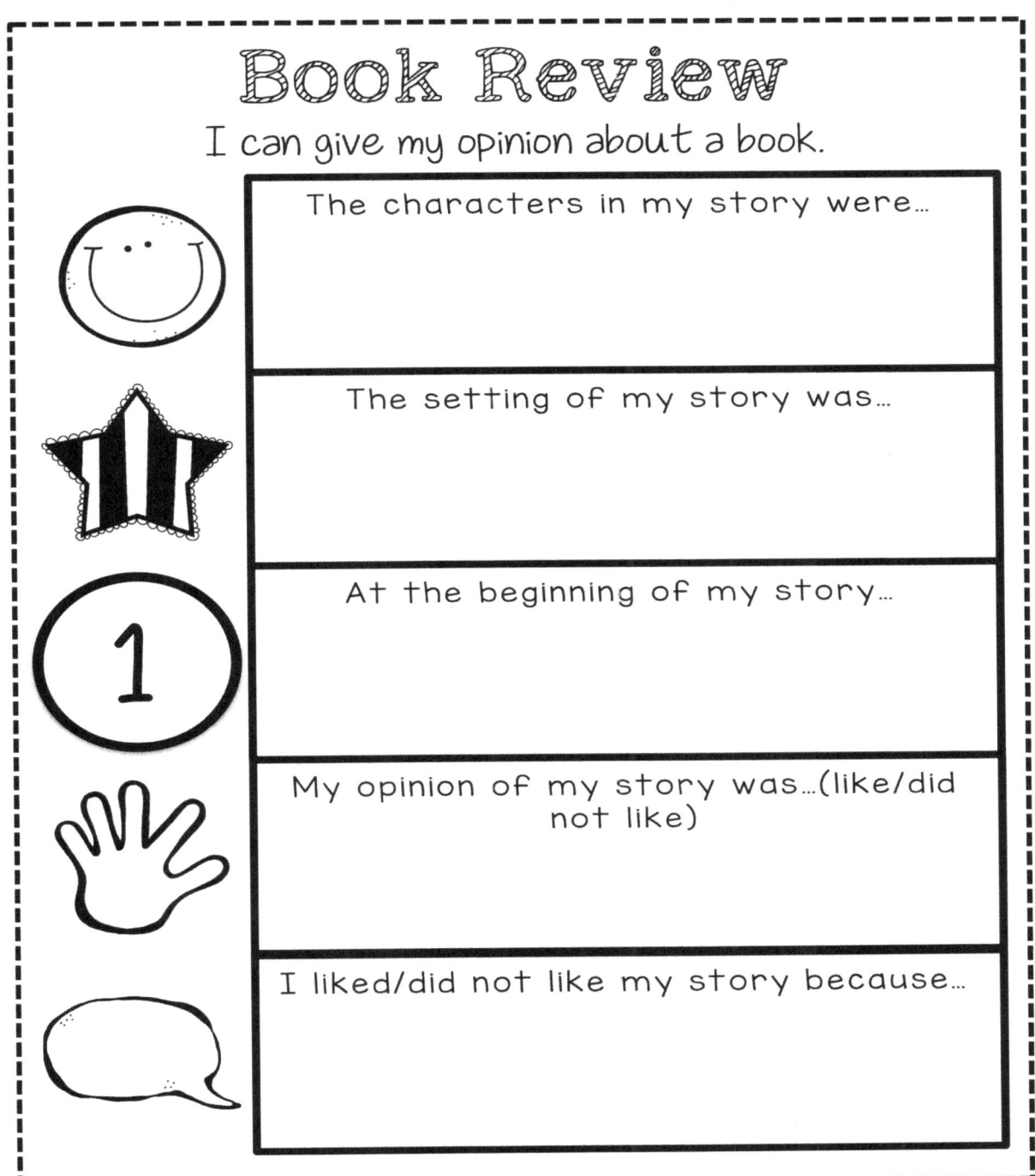

	The characters in my story were…
	The setting of my story was…
	At the beginning of my story…
	My opinion of my story was…(like/did not like)
	I liked/did not like my story because…

© Miss Mack's Kindergarten

Summarizing

Directions: Organize and summarize the important elements and events.

Title and Author

Major Characters

Setting

What is the main conflict?

Main Events

-
-
-
-

How was the main conflict resolved?

Teaching Poetry

Poetry is writing that uses imaginative words to share ideas or emotions, or to tell a story. Students learn so much about language through poetry. They also gain skills in rhyme and meter. The person who writes a poem is called a poet. When teaching poetry to students it would be helpful to utilize the following suggestions:

1. Read the poem aloud to your students.

2. Identify and define words the students do not know.

3. Read the poem aloud again.

4. Summarize the poem.

5. Discuss the poem by asking students if they can make a connection to the poem.

6. Get the students to memorize the poem.

7. Have students recite the poem.

Many of the books that have been presented in previous sections of this resource guide were written as poems. Students will enjoy reading, listening, memorizing, and reciting the following poems written for children by Black authors.

In addition, please be reminded that you can use the same comprehension skills to teach poetry that are used with books and novels. Those skills include: finding the main idea, teaching characterization, making inferences/drawing conclusions, cause and effect, sequencing, compare and contrast, and vocabulary study.

1. *Honey, I Love and Other Poems*

Eloise Greenfield, author

Diane and Leo Dillon, Illustrators

Publisher: HarperCollins, 25th Anniversary Edition, 1986

Genre: Poetry

Summary: In this book, love is demonstrated in many ways as seen through the simple joys of everyday life as expressed by a child through poetry. Children will enjoy listening as they are read. Although the pictures are from the 1970's era, the topics are timeless and precious.

Interest Level: Pre-Kindergarten – Grade 4

Reading Age: 4 – 9 years

2. *Brown Baby Lullaby*

Tameka Fryer Brown, author

A. G. Ford, illustrator

Publisher: Farrar Straus Giroux, New York, 2020

Genre: Children's Poetry/Bedtime Picture Book

Summary: Written for the very young child, this poem tells the story of two parents who lovingly care for their beautiful baby. The skill of sequencing could also be taught using this story that describes a day in the life of a very young child. Loving and caring are themes in this poem.

Interest Level: Pre-Kindergarten – Grade 2

Reading Age: 4 – 7 years

3. *Can't Scare Me* (Trickster Tales)

Ashley Bryan, author and illustrator

Publisher: Atheneum Books for Young Readers, New York, 2013

Genre: Trickster Tale

Summary: This is a tale about a fearless little boy who defies his grandmother's warnings about one, two, and three-headed giants. One day he goes off by himself and he's not scared one bit but realizes he misses his grandma. Read to see what happens next!

Interest Level: Pre-Kindergarten – Grade 4

Reading Age: 4 – 9 years

4. *Legacy* (Women Poets of the Harlem Renaissance)

Nikki Grimes, author

Publisher: Bloomsbury's Children's Books, New York, 2021

Genre: Poetry

Summary: This book consists of nineteen poems written by women of the Harlem Renaissance. It also showcases the work of today's most talented female African American illustrators! Ms. Grimes takes one line from each poem and uses a method called Golden Shovel. One word is written as the last word in the right column and becomes the one line of the poem when read vertically. Similes and metaphors are examples of figurative language found in this book.

Interest Level: Grades 3 – 5

Reading Age: 8 – 10 years

5. *The DreamKeeper and Other Poems*

Langston Hughes, author

Brian Pinkney, illustrator

Publisher: Alfred A. Knopf, 1932 (original publication)

Scholastic, Inc. (First Printing, 1994)

Genre: Poetry

Summary: Written by Langston Hughes, a central figure of the Harlem Renaissance and one of the most influential writers of the twentieth century, this beautiful collection of poetry is about dreams and aspirations. Hughes encourages youth to not abandon their dreams. Children will find that his poetry is as relevant today as when it was written prior to his death in 1967.

Interest Level: Grades 3 – 7

Reading Age: 8 – 12 years

6. *Harlem*

Walter Dean Myers

Christopher Myers, illustrator

Publisher: Scholastic Press, Inc., 1997

Genre: Poetry

Summary: In this poem, the author writes about the history of Harlem, but more importantly about Harlem as a community. He describes a place where people live together, share a culture, and spend time together. Readers will discover what Harlem has meant to African American culture. (This book could also be used as a mentor text to teach setting).

Interest Level: Kindergarten – Grade 5

Reading Age: 5 – 10 years

7. *Ashley Bryan's Puppets*

Ashley Bryan, author

Photographs – Edited by Rich Entel

Publisher: Atheneum Books for Young Readers, New York, 2014

Genre: Poetry

Summary: The author, Ashley Bryan, made hand puppets from raw materials. He created his first puppet at the age of eleven. Each puppet is named for a country in Africa, and the story told by each puppet is set in poetry. The poem written for each puppet describes its role.

Interest Level: Pre-Kindergarten and up

Reading Age: 4 years and up

8. *Jazz*

Walter Dean Myers, author

Christopher Myers, illustrator

Publisher: Holiday House Book, 2006

Genre: Poetry

Summary: Fifteen poems describing jazz and all its elements are found in this wonderful book. Wonderful illustrations of performers and dancers convey the history and depth of this musical style! After reading this book, your students will understand jazz as they have never understood it before!

Interest Level: Grades 3 and up

Reading Age: 8 years and up

9. *My America*

Jan Spivey Gilchrist, author

Ashley Bryan and Jan Spivey Gilchrist, illustrators

Publisher: HarperCollins Publishers, New York, 2007

Genre: Poetry

Summary: This book is a tribute celebrating America's diversity. It is a beautifully written poem that highlights the beauty of America, including its land, water, plants, animals, and most of all, its people.

Interest Level: Pre-Kindergarten – Grade 2

Reading Age: 3 – 8 years

10. *A Place Inside of Me* (A Poem to Heal the Heart)

Zetta Elliott, author

Noa Denmon, illustrator

Publisher: Farrar Strauss Giroux, New York, 2020

Genre: Poetry

Summary: Being loved and accepted for who you are is the theme in this book. It is also a salute to the Black Lives Matter Movement and will assist parents of Black children in explaining the racial strife in this country.

Interest Level: Grades 4 and up

Reading Age: 10 years and up

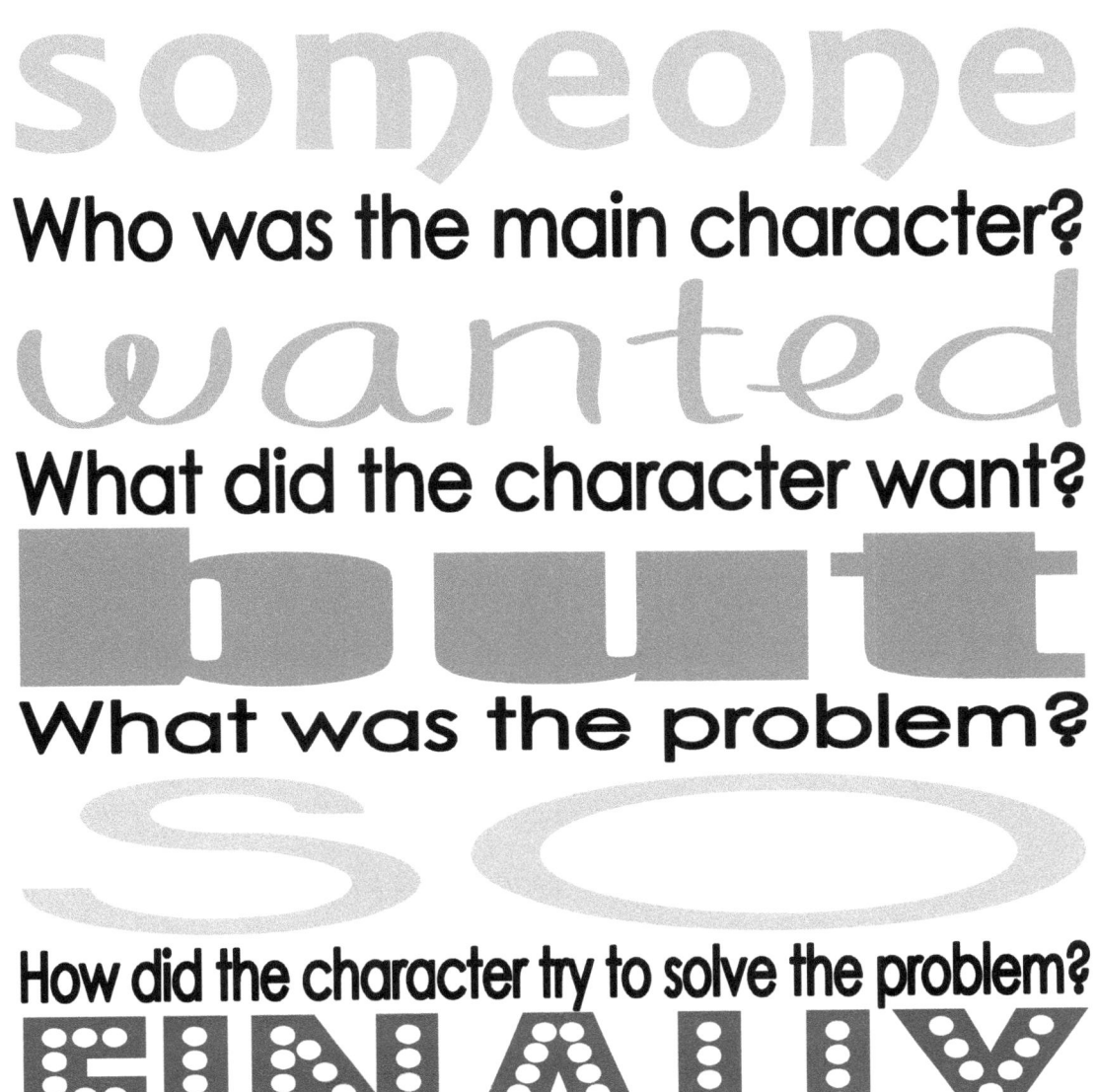

someone
Who was the main character?

wanted
What did the character want?

but
What was the problem?

so
How did the character try to solve the problem?

FINALLY
What was the resolution to the problem?

Index of Titles

Each Kindness (Characterization)

Ella Fitzgerald: The Tale of a Vocal Virtuoso (Sequencing)

Fifty Cents and a Dream (Theme)

Firebird (Figurative Language)

For the Love of the Game (Characterization)

Freedom in Congo Square (Setting)

Freedom Over Me (Eleven Slaves, Their Lives and Dreams Brought to Life) (Author's Purpose)

Freedom Soup (Sequencing)

Freedom's School (Cause and Effect)

Gifted Hands, Revised Kidz Edition, The Ben Carson Story (Novels and Chapter Books) (Novels and Nonfiction Books)

Gifts Are Given with Love (Characterization)

Gordon Parks (How the Photographer Captured Black and White America) (Cause and Effect)

Harlem (Poetry)

Harlem Renaissance Party (Setting)

He's Got the Whole World in His Hands (Theme)

Hidden Figures – Four Black Women and the Space Race (Characterization)

Honey, I Love and Other Poems (Poetry)

I am Brown (Vocabulary)

I Am Enough (Characterization)

I Believe (Theme)

I Got Next (Characterization)

I'm Gonna Push Through (Characterization)

Jazz (Poetry)

Jesse Owens – Legendary Track Star (Characterization, Sequencing)

Jump at the Sun (Sequencing)

Just a Lucky So and So (Figurative Language)

Just Like a Mama (Compare and Contrast, Figurative Language)

Just the Two of Us (Main Idea)

Kamala Harris (Rooted in Justice) (Sequencing)

Kid President's Guide to Being Awesome (Author's Purpose)

Legacy (Women Poets of the Harlem Renaissance) (Poetry)

Little Dreamers – Visionary Women Around the World (Characterization)

Mae Among the Stars (Sequencing)

Marian Anderson (A Great Singer) (Sequencing)

Mary McLeod Bethune (A Great American Educator) (Sequencing)

More Than Anything Else (Cause and Effect)

Moses (When Harriet Led Her People to Freedom) (Theme)

Mufaro's Beautiful Daughters (Characterization)

My America (Poetry)

My Brother Charlie (Author's Purpose, Compare and Contrast)

Neeny Coming, Neeny Going (Setting)

Nelson Mandela (Theme)

Not Quite Snow White (Main Idea)

Of Thee I Sing (Characterization)

Off to See the Sea (Author's Purpose)

One Crazy Summer (Novels)

Pecan Pie Baby (Compare and Contrast)

Please, Puppy, Please (Cause and Effect)

Preaching to the Chickens – The Story of Young John Lewis (Sequencing)

Rhythm Ride (A Road Through the Motown Sound) (Sequencing)

Roll of Thunder, Hear My Cry (Author's Purpose, Novels)

Rosa (Main Idea, Cause and Effect)

Ruby Bridges Goes to School (My True Story) (Characterization)

Ruth and the Green Book (Author's Purpose)

Salt in His Shoes (Characterization)

Sisters and Champions (The True Story of Venus and Serena Williams)

Sit-In: How Four Friends Stood Up By Sitting Down (Setting)

Sojourner Truth's Step-Stomp Stride (Theme)

Sulwe (Cause and Effect)

Talk About a Family (Making Inferences/Drawing Conclusions)

Tar Beach (Making Inferences/Drawing Conclusions)

The Animal Market (Author's Purpose)

The Bell Rang (Sequencing)

The Bench (Theme)

The Day You Begin (Compare and Contrast)

The DreamKeeper and Other Poems (Poetry)

The Gold Cadillac (Making Inferences/Drawing Conclusions)

The Hundred Penny Box (Making Inferences/Drawing Conclusions)

The Magician's Hat (Making Inferences/Drawing Conclusions)

The Mighty Miss Malone (Novels)

The Patchwork Quilt (Making Inferences/Drawing Conclusions)

The People Could Fly (The Picture Book) (Main Idea)

The Undefeated (Characterization, Vocabulary)

The Watsons Go to Birmingham – 1963 (Novels)

This is the Rope (Sequencing, Cause and Effect)

Time for Kenny (Sequencing, Vocabulary)

Trombone Shorty (Cause and Effect)

We Are the Ship (The Story of Negro League Baseball) (Nonfiction Text Features)

We Beat the Street (How a Friendship Pact Led to Success) (Novels and Nonfiction Books)

We Came to America (Main Idea)

Why Should I Go to School? (Cause and Effect)

Why the Sun and the Moon Live in the Sky (Cause and Effect)

William and the Good Old Days (Main Idea)

Index of Black Authors and Illustrators

Jordan, Roslyn

Joy, Angela

Lee, Spike

Lee, Tonya Lewis

Lent, Blair

Lopez, Rafael

Mathis, Sandra Pierce

Mathis, Sharon

McKissack, Frederick

McKissack, Patricia

Meghan, Duchess of Sussex

Mildred Taylor

Miller, Sharee

Milner, Deneen

Mitchell, Malcolm

Miyares, Daniel

Montague, Brad

Myers, Christopher

Myers, Nneka

Myers, Walter Dean

Nelson, Kadir

Novak, Robby

Nyong'o, Lupita

Obama, Barack

Peete, Holly Robinson

Peete, Ryan Elizabeth

Peoples, Daria

Pinkney, Andrea Davis

Pinkney, Brian

Pinkney, Jerry

Ramsey, Calvin Alexander
(with Gwen Strauss)

Ransome, James

Redd, Nancy

Ringgold, Faith

Robinson, Christian

Shetterley, Margot

Smith, Will

Steptoe, John

Valdez, Marisa

Weatherford, Carole Boston

Wilkins, Joyce R.

Williams, Alicia

Woodson, Jacqueline

Wright, Jasmyn

Wright, Shannon

About the Author

Sandra Pierce Mathis received a Doctor of Education in Educational Leadership and Policy Studies from The George Washington University in Washington, DC. She also earned undergraduate and graduate degrees in Special Education and an Advanced Study Certificate in Supervision from Old Dominion University in Norfolk, Virginia. A 45-year veteran educator born and raised in Surry County, Virginia, Dr. Mathis has resided in the City of Virginia Beach, Virginia, for many years.

Having served in five different public school divisions, a private hospital setting, and as a full-time Associate Professor in Special Education at Norfolk State University, all in the state of Virginia, Dr. Mathis has gained a great deal of experience and recognizes the need for quality literacy instruction for children. Finally, Dr. Mathis is the published author of four books and loves to read, write, garden, bake, and take walks. She is the mother of one extraordinary daughter who learned to read at a very early age!